The Open University
LIVING WITH TECHNOLOGY
A Foundation Course

PLAIN ENGLISH

Prepared by the Course Team

D0434148

The Open University Press

The members of the *Living with Technology* Course Team acknowledge the generous help we have received in preparing *Plain English* from Diané Collinson, Staff Tutor and Senior Lecturer in Philosophy, Faculty of Arts.

Written by Diané Collinson, Gillian Kirkup, Robin Kyd and Lynne Slocombe

The Open University, Walton Hall, Milton Keynes, MK7 6AA

First published 1979. Second edition 1982. Reprinted with corrections 1983

Copyright © 1979, 1982 The Open University

All rights reserved. No part of this work may be reproduced in any form, by mimeograph or any other means, without permission in writing from the publisher

Designed by the Graphic Design Group of the Open University

Printed in Great Britain by Spottiswoode Ballantyne Limited, Colchester and London

ISBN 0 335 08982 8

This text forms part of an Open University Course. A complete list of mainstream and tributary texts is given at the end of this text

For general availability of supporting material referred to in this text please write to: Open University Educational Enterprises Ltd, 12 Cofferidge Close, Stony Stratford, Milton Keynes, MK11 1BY, Great Britain

Further information on Open University courses may be obtained from: The Admissions Office, The Open University, PO Box 48, Walton Hall, Milton Keynes, MK7 6AB

2.2

Contents

Introduction

Plain English developed out of an idea that began in the Open University's South-West Region. There, some years ago, five part-time arts tutors joined with Diané Collinson to produce a set of work-books for students who had been out of touch with formal education for some time and wanted to revise or learn some basic writing skills. These work-books were known as *Open Daily*. While we, the *Living with Technology* Course Team, were developing our new foundation course we heard of *Open Daily* and decided to use and adapt it for our own students. The result is *Plain English*.

It opens with an 'Introductory quiz' and then is divided into five main sections, each containing exercises on a particular topic. The sections 'Punctuation', 'Spelling', 'Grammar' and 'Style' are divided into 'days' and the idea is that you should work through them a day at a time. Each 'day' should give you about fifteen or twenty minutes' work. On some days, particularly in the 'Spelling' section, you may find you spend less time than this; on other days (e.g. 'cliché' in the 'Style' section) you may need to spend a little longer to absorb the material. The last section, 'Bibliographies and References', is a little different. It is not divided into 'days'. You may find it most useful to refer to this section later on during your study of *Living with Technology*; its subject is one of those things that academics assume you know about already, yet they're not always quite clear about themselves. Answers are provided for all the exercises.

Plain English has been designed to offer you a programme of work that will not encroach too much on your routine study time. Most of the 'days' can be worked over a cup of coffee or on a train journey. None of the exercises need be undertaken in isolation; your friends or family may enjoy helping or offering a solution.

Doing the 'Introductory quiz' should help you in two ways. First, it will give you an idea of what subject matter is covered in *Plain English*. Secondly, it should help you to decide which of the sections will be of help to you. You can do the quiz on your own or at a group session with your tutor–counsellor. The answers to the quiz follow immediately after it.

If you then decide to tackle any of the sections, I should like to suggest the following:

First, please try to work steadily through the whole section on a regular daily basis. Tackle the work carefully, use a dictionary when it is recommended and don't look up the answers until you've made a thorough attempt to answer the whole exercise.

Secondly, be alert to everything you read, from advertisements to textbooks, to see if it is clear, accurate and concise in a way that is appropriate to it. Clear writing shows clear thinking.

Thirdly, do try to talk to family, friends and fellow students about the exercises. This will help you not only to enjoy the exercises, but also to remember them.

If you have time, please send us your comments on and criticisms of *Plain English* so that it can be improved for future use. Write to Robin Kyd, Senior Editor, Faculty of Technology, The Open University, Walton Hall, Milton Keynes, MK7 6AA.

I hope you will find as much enjoyment and profit in working through *Plain English* as its team of writers found in producing it.

A note about your dictionary

You probably already have a dictionary in your home, but you might like to consider whether it will be adequate for the sort of use you will want to make of it during your career as a university student. If you don't have a dictionary, you really ought to buy one right away.

In *Living with Technology* the Course Team is taking seriously the task of *teaching* you all the technical terms that you will need in order to write about the issues and topics covered in the course. So you should not need a specialist technical dictionary to help you understand the technical terms in *Living with Technology*, even if you feel you have little or no technical background. What you will need a dictionary for is to look up the meanings of any unfamiliar non-technical words that you may come across in your reading, to check that you are using a word in its proper sense and, above all, to check on the spelling of words you want to use in your own writing.

I should like to encourage you to keep your dictionary handy when you are studying and to dip into it whenever you come across a new or unfamiliar word. If you are at all unsure of your spelling, make full use of your dictionary when writing your assignments.

Details of some dictionaries are given in the second part of the Bibliography to *Plain English*. The dictionaries listed are simply examples from the many available; no recommendation is implied by their inclusion in the list. If you are going to buy a dictionary, I suggest you browse through the dictionary section of your nearest large bookshop. Two points I shall make here. First, a pocket-sized dictionary will probably not be comprehensive enough for your needs; my own preference would be for a dictionary of the size and scope of *Chambers Twentieth Century Dictionary* or the *Concise Oxford Dictionary*. The second point is that you should be buying your dictionary with a view to *using* it frequently over a period of years. Bearing this in mind you should think very carefully before buying a paperback dictionary rather than a hard-backed one.

Introductory quiz

This quiz consists of thirty-seven examples of incorrect, sloppy or thoughtless English.

For each example, please do three things:

Spot the fault and encircle it.

Briefly describe what is wrong.

Wherever possible, write a correct or improved version.

Note

Describing exactly what is wrong can be difficult. You are not expected to give full technical descriptions of grammatical and other errors. It will be quite enough to say such things as 'grammar wrong', 'meaning confused', 'punctuation wrong', 'spelling wrong' and so on. Most of the examples present outright errors for you to spot and correct, but a few are instances of bad style (cliché, jargon, wordiness, etc.) and you may feel it not worth while trying to rewrite one or two of these examples. Indeed, the point about bad style is that it hides the writer's meaning, so that a reader cannot know for certain what the writer meant. So, in the case of really bad style, you simply won't be able to decide what the correct version is.

1   I have now discussed the proposal for restocking all 500 deep freezers with my colleagues.

Fault

Correction

2   He was definately on the wrong side of the law.

Fault

Correction

3   Today pneumatic tyres are fitted to practically all road vehicles, originally they were developed for use on bicycles.

Fault

Correction

4   When the heyday of science-fiction and horror films is over.

Fault

Correction

5   The development of breeder reactors completely change the economics of ore extraction and boost the known reserves of nuclear energy very considerably.

Fault

Correction

6   Neither knowledge nor skill are needed.

Fault

Correction

7   The project, having been approved, the firm began to recruit the necessary staff.

Fault

Correction

8   There were less visitors than usual.

Fault

Correction

8

9   The seminar ended by an open discussion.

Fault

Correction

10   The decision to computerize the accounting system has badly effected our relations with our customers.

Fault

Correction

11   The driver of a car, which does not comply with these regulations, is liable to a fine or imprisonment.

Fault

Correction

12   Many birds are protected by law nowadays, i.e. the osprey, the golden eagle, the buzzard and the bittern.

Fault

Correction

13   Manufacturors of toys have a responsibility to make them safe.

Fault

Correction

14   The remuneration received by the subordinate officials of this
organization exceeds by a very considerable proportion what is generally
placed on offer by other comparable firms.

Fault

Correction

15   This drug has proved successful in a percentage of cases.

Fault

Correction

16   Organizational structure must provide for the co-ordination of
functions and activities in order that interdependent members of the
organization and subunits interact in harmony with each other and with
other sectors and activities of society in the achievement of the
organization's goals and objectives and the delivery of the services it
provides.

Fault

Correction

17   The vehicle has it's own reserve power supply.

Fault

Correction

18   His condition can only be alleviated by drugs.

Fault

Correction

19   After adding carefully a few drops of anti-foam oil, the bubbles disappear.

Fault

Correction

20   Their five-year mission was to boldly go where no man had gone before.

Fault

Correction

21   We immediately contacted anyone whom we suspected had received a faulty vehicle.

Fault

Correction

22   It is necessary to forecast the number, duration and geographical distribution of telephone calls, usually referred to as the telephone traffic in six or seven years' time.

Fault

Correction

23   In this day and age, while industry is grinding to a halt, one can feel the wind of change heralding the arrival of a new climate of opinion.

Fault

Correction

24   I have outlined below the reasons that have led to them being given
appointments in these departments.

Fault

Correction

25   The new parameters for the jobs of the employees were fully
described to them by the director.

Fault

Correction

26   Data that is more than five years old is of limited use.

Fault

Correction

27   The houses erected should be broken down into types.

Fault

Correction

28   The corporation has not asked for any advice and I do not doubt
its ability to deal with the immediate situation themselves.

Fault

Correction

29   He has been more successful than me.

Fault

Correction

12

30   I practiced at the terminal for several hours each week.

Fault

Correction

31   How will a driver – of a furniture van – on a motorway – perform in a strong – gusting side-wind?

Fault

Correction

32   The minister agreed in principle to a new urban public transport system development plan.

Fault

Correction

33   There were yellow lines down all the streets and the car parks were full, so I couldn't find nowhere to park the car.

Fault

Correction

34   The cause of the delay in laying the foundations was due to exceptionally heavy rain flooding the area.

Fault

Correction

35   One short inspection was not enough to assertain the extent of the damage.

Fault

Correction

36   It was certainly him, and not the owner of the car, who now came running along the drive.

Fault

Correction

37   When the scheme is finished all local roads will connect up with the main relief road.

Fault

Correction

Answers to introductory quiz

1   I have now discussed the proposal for restocking all 500 deep freezers (with my colleagues.)

Fault   Wrong position of words (Grammar)
Correction   I have now discussed with my colleagues the proposal for restocking all 500 deep freezers.

2   He was (definately) on the wrong side of the law.

Fault   Spelling
Correction   He was definitely on the wrong side of the law.

3   Today pneumatic tyres are fitted to practically all road vehicles(,) originally they were developed for use on bicycles.

Fault   Inadequate comma (Punctuation)
Correction   Today pneumatic tyres are fitted to practically all road vehicles; originally they were developed for use on bicycles.

4   (When the heyday of science-fiction and horror films is over.)

Fault   Not a sentence (Grammar)
Correction   e.g. I shall be glad when the heyday of science-fiction and horror films is over.

5   The development of breeder reactors completely (change) the economics of extraction and (boost) the known reserves of nuclear energy very considerably.

Fault   Grammar wrong
Correction   The development of breeder reactors completely changes the economics of ore extraction and boosts the known reserves of nuclear energy very considerably.

6   Neither knowledge nor skill (are) needed.

Fault   Grammar wrong
Correction   Neither knowledge nor skill is needed.

7   The project(,) having been approved, the firm began to recruit the necessary staff.

Fault   Wrongly inserted comma (Punctuation)
Correction   The project having been approved, the firm began to recruit the necessary staff.

8   There were ⌈ less ⌉ visitors than usual.

Fault   Wrong use of *less* with *visitors* (Grammar)
Correction   There were fewer visitors than usual.

9   The seminar ended ⌈ by ⌉ an open discussion.

Fault   Wrong word (Grammar)
Correction   The seminar ended with an open discussion.

10   The decision to computerize the accounting system has badly ⌈ effected ⌉ our relations with our customers.

Fault   Wrong word: confusion of *affect* and *effect* (Grammar)
Correction   The decision to computerize the accounting system has badly affected our relations with our customers.

11   The driver of a car, which does not comply with these regulations, is liable to a fine or imprisonment.

Fault   Wrongly inserted commas (Punctuation)
Correction   The driver of a car which does not comply with these regulations is liable to a fine or imprisonment.

12   Many birds are protected by law nowadays, ⌈ i.e. ⌉ the osprey, the golden eagle, the buzzard and the bittern.

Fault   Wrong use of i.e. (that is) (Style)
Correction   Many birds are protected by law nowadays, e.g. (for example) the osprey, the golden eagle, the buzzard and the bittern.

13 ⌈ Manufacturors ⌉ of toys have a responsibility to make them safe.

Fault   Spelling
Correction   Manufacturers of toys have a responsibility to make them safe.

14   The remuneration received by the subordinate officials of this organization exceeds by a very considerable proportion what is generally placed on offer by other comparable firms.

Fault   Pompous and jargonistic (Style)
Correction   Compared with similar firms, this one pays its junior employees a lot.

15   This drug has proved successful in a (percentage) of cases.

Fault   Meaningless use of percentage (Style)
Correction   This drug has proved successful in a large (small?) proportion of cases.

16   Organizational structure must provide for the co-ordination of functions and activities in order that interdependent members of the organization and subunits interact in harmony with each other and with other sectors and activities of society in the achievement of the organization's goals and objectives and the delivery of the services it provides.

Fault   Jargon (Style)
Correction   The organization must have a structure that enables all its members to work together to achieve its aims.

17   The vehicle has (it's) own reserve power supply.

Fault   Wrong use of apostrophe (Punctuation)
Correction   The vehicle has its own reserve power supply.

18   His condition can (only) be alleviated by drugs.

Fault   Ambiguous placing of *only* (Grammar)
Correction   Only drugs can alleviate his condition.
Or: Drugs can only alleviate (but not cure) his condition.

19   (After adding) carefully a few drops of anti-foam oil, the bubbles disappear.

Fault   Grammar wrong
Correction   After a few drops of anti-foam oil have been carefully added, the bubbles disappear.

20   Their five-year mission was (to boldly go) where no man had gone before.

Fault   Split infinitive (Grammar)
Correction   Their five-year mission was to go boldly where no man had gone before.

21   We immediately contacted anyone (whom) we suspected had received a faulty vehicle.

Fault   *Whom* for *who* (Grammar)
Correction   We immediately contacted anyone who we suspected had received a faulty vehicle.

22   It is necessary to forecast the number, duration and geographical distribution of telephone calls, usually referred to as the telephone traffic◯in six or seven years' time.

Fault   Comma missing (Punctuation)
Correction   It is necessary to forecast the number, duration and geographical distribution of telephone calls, usually referred to as the telephone traffic, in six or seven years' time.

23   In this day and age, while industry is grinding to a halt, one can feel the wind of change heralding the arrival of a new climate of opinion.

Fault   Clichés throughout (Style)
Correction   Industry is not thriving nowadays and one senses change that will introduce new ideas.

24   I have outlined below the reasons that have led to (them) being given appointments in these departments.

Fault   Grammar wrong
Correction   I have outlined below the reasons which have led to their being given appointments in these departments.

25   The new (parameters) for the jobs of the employees were fully described to them by the director.

Fault   Incorrect use of technical (mathematical) term (Style)
Correction   The employees were given a full description of their new job specifications by the director.

26   Data that (is) more than five years old (is) of limited use.

Fault   Grammar wrong
Correction   Data that are more than five years old are of limited use.

27 The houses erected should be (broken down) into types.

Fault Ludicrous effect of metaphor (Style)
Correction The houses erected should be classified according to type.

28 The corporation (has) not asked for any advice and I do not doubt (its) ability to deal with the immediate situation (themselves.)

Fault Grammar wrong
Correction The corporation has not asked for any advice and
I do not doubt its ability to deal with the immediate situation itself.
Or: The corporation have not asked for any advice and I do not doubt
their ability to deal with the immediate situation themselves.

29 He has been more successful than (me.)

Fault Grammar wrong
Correction He has been more successful than I (have)

30 I (practiced) at the terminal for several hours each week.

Fault Wrong spelling
Correction I practised at the terminal for several hours each week.

31 How will a driver (–) of a furniture van (–) on a motorway (–) perform in a strong (–) gusting side-wind?

Fault Unnecessary dashes (Punctuation)
Correction How will a driver of a furniture van on a motorway perform in a strong gusting side-wind?

32 The minister agreed in principle to a (new urban public transport system development plan.)

Fault Bad use of nouns as adjectives (Style)
Correction The minister agreed in principle to a new plan for developing a system of public transport in the city.

33 There were yellow lines down all the streets and the car parks were full, so I (couldn't find nowhere) to park the car.

Fault   Double negative (Grammar)
Correction   There were yellow lines down all the streets and the car parks were full, so I couldn't find anywhere to park the car.
Or: ... so I could find nowhere to park the car.

34   The (cause) of the delay in laying the foundations (was due) to exceptionally heavy rain flooding the area.

Fault   Redundancy (Style)
Correction   The cause of the delay in laying the foundations was the exceptionally heavy rain flooding the area.
Or: The delay in laying the foundations was due to exceptionally heavy rain flooding the area.

35   One short inspection was not enough to (assertain) the extent of the damage.

Fault   Spelling
Correction   One short inspection was not enough to ascertain the extent of the damage.

36   It was certainly (him), and not the owner of the car, who now came running along the drive.

Fault   Grammar wrong
Correction   It was certainly he, and not the owner of the car, who now came running along the drive.

37   When the scheme is finished all local roads will connect (up) with the main relief road.

Fault   Redundant word (Grammar)
Correction   When the scheme is finished all local roads will connect with the main relief road.

Punctuation

Day one

Full stop

1   The full stop is used to mark the end of all sentences except direct questions (?) or exclamations (!). A capital letter, of course, is used to mark the beginning of all sentences.

You should have no difficulty with the full stop.

Exercise 1

To start you off handling punctuation confidently, add *full stops* and capitals to this passage, which contains five sentences. No other punctuation is needed.

Brunel's critics still refused to be convinced and now maintained that when the time came to remove the centering altogether the bridge would surely collapse the engineer himself had no doubts whatever about his bridge but he ruled that the centres should not be removed finally until it had stood through another winter the suspicion that this was due not so much to excessive caution as to an impish sense of humour is hard to resist certainly the fact that the bridge was standing entirely free for nine months while his jealous opponents supposed that the centering was still helping to support it was a joke that Brunel must have relished keenly its point was revealed and his critics confounded by a violent storm one autumn night in 1839 which blew all the useless centering down

---

2   You also find the full stop used with initials and abbreviations.

For example:

> I.K. Brunel, e.g., ed. (editor), p. (page), ch. (chapter), no. (number), vol. (volume), a.m., p.m., co., e.m.f. (electromotive force), etc.

You may be puzzled by some modern practices relating to the omission of full stops with contractions and capital initials. If so, do not spend time trying to fathom out the rules. It is now quite common and acceptable to omit full stops from capital initials such as BBC, UK, OU, VHF, DDT,

CEGB, and this is the style normally used in Open University publications. But, if you prefer to use full stops, that is still perfectly acceptable. Also, full stops are now commonly omitted from contractions (i.e. shortenings of words that keep the final letter of the whole word) like Dr, Mrs, 3rd edn (third edition). Again, if you think this is an unnecessary distinction, you are free to write contractions with full stops.

Exercise 2

Add full stops to these sentences:

(a) Mr and Mrs J B Jones, who live at 23 St James's Gardens, told P C Alderbank that they had been woken at 3 a m by the sound of glass breaking and had seen a man running out of the house opposite, no 26

(b) Radio programmes for the OU are broadcast on VHF only; TV programmes are broadcast on either BBC2 or BBC1

(c) In March 1979 the Royal Society held a discussion meeting on nuclear magnetic resonance (nmr) of intact biological systems organized by Prof R J P Williams, FRS, Prof E R Andrew and Dr G K Radda

---

3   You do need to know, however, that it is incorrect to add a full stop to the *symbol* for a unit of measurement or for a chemical element. Here are some examples:

m	metre	C	carbon
kg	kilogram	Fe	iron
V	volt	U	uranium

Capitals

1   As already mentioned, a capital letter is used to mark the beginning of each sentence. Try therefore to avoid opening a sentence with numerals or symbols.

2   Capitals are used for the first letters of the names of people, places, months, days of the week, etc. They are also used for the first letters of all the main words in the titles of organizations, people, books, periodicals or journals, newspapers, etc. Here are just a few examples:

the Open University, the Bishop of Oxford, *Animal Farm*, *Journal of Materials Science, Daily Telegraph.*

3   The old rule of using a capital letter for the particular and a small letter for the general is still a helpful guide. For example:

> Heathrow Airport is one of the world's busiest international airports.

> The figures in this book are excellent; Figure 14, for example, shows all the complexity of a modern telecommunication network without being cluttered with unnecessary detail.

In general, avoid unnecessary use of capitals and be consistent throughout your writing.

Exercise 3

Mark the letters in this passage that are incorrectly or inconsistently capitalized. Also add capitals where necessary.

within the wider community of british universities the Open University is the only Institution that demands no Entrance Qualifications of its Students. this means, however, that Foundation courses have to play a crucial role in its teaching system. They form the bridge between students of enormously varied Educational backgrounds and the Higher-level Courses that will enable them to become Graduates.

In designing *Living with Technology* the Course Team paid almost as much attention to the Course's role as a foundation course as to the fact that it is a course about *Technology*.

You should beware of one or two traps when writing about technical subjects. I shall deal with these in what follows.

4   Do not be misled into thinking that, because a recognized set of initials is in capitals, the term itself takes capitals. Here are some examples:

AM	amplitude modulation,
PVC	polyvinyl chloride,
RAM	random-access memory,
TNT	trinitrotoluene,
UHF	ultra-high frequency.

Perhaps the best example to keep in mind is TV.

5   Before you are introduced in *Living with Technology* to units of measurement, chemical elements and their symbols, let me tell you straight away that capitals are *not* used for the first letters of the names of

units of measurement or of chemical elements and compounds. You will know at least some of the names of units of measurement used by technologists:

second, kilogram, volt, watt, ampere, metre.

The point to note here is that none of them has a capital first letter, even though many of them are taken from personal names. The watt, for example, is named after James Watt (1736–1819).

Even if you are not at all sure what a chemical element is, you are familiar with the names of several:

iron, aluminium, iodine, tin, neon, arsenic, oxygen, copper, hydrogen, uranium, plutonium, silver, gold.

You are probably familiar with the names of at least a few chemical compounds, for example:

carbon dioxide, sulphuric acid, butane, sodium chloride.

None of them requires a capital letter.

Exercise 4

Add *capitals* and full stops to this passage, which contains six sentences. All other punctuation is supplied.

the castner cell underwent various slight modifications during the first quarter of the century, but in 1924 the american j c downs patented a cell for the production of sodium from fused sodium chloride this consisted of a steel tank lined with firebrick containing a massive cylindrical graphite anode projecting through the base, surrounded coaxially by a cathode of iron gauze by adding calcium chloride to the sodium chloride, the melting-point of the electrolyte is reduced from 800 °C to 505 °C the energy efficiency of the downs cell process from salt to sodium is about three times greater than that of the composite process of first producing sodium hydroxide in a mercury cell, followed by further electrolysis in a castner cell however, both processes were in operation in 1950 the price of sodium in the usa dropped from $2.00 per pound in 1890 to $0.15 per pound in 1946

Day two

Comma

For the full stop I was able to give you a simple, definite rule about its use at the end of sentences. There are no equally straightforward rules for all the various uses of the comma. Putting a comma in, or leaving one out, at a particular place in a sentence may not be a matter of right or wrong punctuation. The comma may simply give part of the sentence a different emphasis, or it may change the meaning of the sentence. The decision to use the comma will then depend on exactly what it is you want to say. There is also some room for personal preference in the use of commas, with one writer putting commas in where another would leave them out. Nevertheless, the following examples show you some of the uses to which commas are put.

1   To separate items in a list:

> The correct use of the comma – if there is such a thing as 'correct' use – can only be acquired by common sense, observation and taste. (E. Gowers, *The Complete Plain Words*, 2nd edn, Penguin, 1973, p. 242.)

> The engine, the gearbox, the clutch and the brakes had all been repaired.

or   The engine, the gearbox, the clutch, and the brakes had all been repaired.

In this sentence the comma before *and* is optional; in other lists a comma before the final *and* may be needed to avoid ambiguity:

> Shops that will be opening in the centre include branches of Boots, W.H. Smith, Marks and Spencer, and Woolworths.

Exercise 5

Put commas in the following sentences:

(a) Your home might be heated by solid fuel oil gas or electricity.

(b) Resources are defined as energy materials labour and capital.

(c) He found he needed several metres of electric cable three junction boxes a packet of insulated staples four light switches and an assortment of tools.

---

2   To separate descriptive words when several are used together:

> Glass is a hard, brittle, transparent material.
>
> Dinneford's Gripe Mixture quickly, gently brings up wind.

Notice that commas are not required in this next example:

> This important new discovery was reported in a recent scientific paper.

Can you see why commas are used in the first two examples, but not in this last one? In the next two sentences the difference should be clearer:

> The new experimental procedures are intended to improve safety in the laboratory.
>
> This new, experimental traffic scheme will operate for one month initially.

In the first sentence 'new experimental procedures' implies that there were old experimental procedures, but in the second sentence the suggestion is that the old traffic scheme was not experimental. Without the comma, 'new' describes 'experimental procedures'; with the comma, 'new' describes only the 'traffic scheme'. Another way of looking at it is this: when descriptive words are separated by commas, they each act independently on the word they are describing.

Exercise 6

Add commas where appropriate:

(a) Copper is a malleable ductile metal.

(b) Many new electronic gadgets have appeared in recent years.

(c) The new crystals tended to be long smooth whip-like filaments.

---

3   To separate a sequence of closely related clauses:

> Oxygen and nitrogen are gases, nearly all the metallic elements are solids, but of all the chemical elements only bromine and mercury are liquids at room temperature.
>
> Put the peeled potatoes into a pan, cover them with cold water, add a pinch of salt and boil for 15–20 minutes.
>
> Water evaporates from the oceans, forms clouds in the atmosphere, falls as rain, drains from the land as surface water into the rivers and flows back into the oceans.

A clause, by the way, is simply a part of a sentence that has a verb in it, and a verb is a 'doing' or 'being' word, like *are, put, boil, evaporates, flows* in the above examples.

Sometimes there are just two clauses, joined by a word like *but, or* or *and*:

> Swan's first carbon-filament lamp was made in 1848, but its life was too brief to be useful.

> Shortly afterwards Francis Hauksbee demonstrated that charged bodies repel as well as attract each other, and in 1729 Stephen Gray made the very important contribution of distinguishing between conductors (mainly metals) and non-conductors. (T.K. Derry and T.I. Williams, *A Short History of Technology*, Oxford University Press, paperback edn, 1970, pp. 608–9.)

Nearly always a comma is put before *but* or *or* joining two clauses. A comma is preferable before an *and* that joins two lengthy clauses (as in the last example), but a comma is not required before the *and* joining two short clauses:

> I went to the library and I borrowed a book on astronomy.

When both clauses have the same subject, as here (*I*), the subject is often left out the second time:

> I went to the library and borrowed a book on astronomy.

A common mis-use of the comma is to separate two main clauses that are not linked by a word like 'and'. Here is an example of this mis-use:

> Cellulose forms the main constituent of plant-cell walls and textile fibres, it is an example of a natural polymer.

The comma is inadequate here. A stronger break is required than a comma gives, and this sentence would be better punctuated with a semicolon:

> Cellulose forms the main constituent of plant-cell walls and textile fibres; it is an example of a natural polymer.

You will be dealing with the semicolon more fully in Day three. For the present I just want you to be on your guard against using the comma for a job that it is not strong enough to tackle.

Another common mistake is to place a single comma between a subject and its verb. Here are two examples of this wrong use of a comma:

> Many new electronic gadgets, have appeared in recent years.

The construction of the new furnace, was completed ahead of
schedule.

Although the single comma is wrong here, you will see in Day four that a
pair of commas enclosing a word or words may be placed in this
position.

Exercise 7

Add commas where appropriate to these sentences:

(a) The engine stalled the brakes failed and the car started to roll
backwards.

(b) Britain now has a system as advanced as any in the world and other
countries are adopting similar measures.

(c) I was finding it hard to keep up with the course and had missed one
or two television programmes but I made a point of going to all the
tutorials and sending in my assignments on time.

(d) Seaside habitats are equally rich and provide great contrasts in
species.

Exercise 8 (revision)

Add *commas*, capitals and full stops to these passages:

(a) all matter is made up of atoms and all atoms are made up of an inner
nucleus (plural: nuclei) surrounded by electrons almost the whole mass of
the atom is concentrated in the nucleus but the nucleus is much smaller
than the whole atom the bulk of the nucleus is made up of protons and
neutrons all the atoms of a particular chemical element contain the same
number of protons and this number is known as the atomic number of the
element the atomic number of hydrogen is 1 that of carbon is 6 and that
of oxygen is 8 this means that all hydrogen atoms contain 1 proton all
carbon atoms contain 6 protons and all oxygen atoms contain 8 protons

(b) the pressure volume and temperature of a fixed quantity of gas are
interrelated boyle's law states that at constant temperature the volume of
a given mass of gas is inversely proportional to the pressure and charles's
law states that at constant pressure the volume of a given mass of gas is
directly proportional to the absolute temperature for a mole of gas these
two laws may be combined in the gas equation $pV = RT$ in this equation
p is the pressure V is the volume R is the gas constant and T is the

absolute temperature gases do not strictly obey the gas laws but follow them more and more closely as the pressure of the gas is reduced

You will be looking at more uses of the comma in Days four and six.

Day three

Semicolon

Study this quotation carefully:

> Do not be afraid of the semicolon; it can be most useful. It marks a longer pause, a more definite break in the sense, than the comma; at the same time it says 'Here is a clause or sentence too closely related to what has gone before to be cut off by a full stop'. The semicolon is a stronger version of the comma. (*The Complete Plain Words*, p. 261.)

This quotation is worth noting; it summarizes well what you need to know about the semicolon.

Exercise 9

In each of the following sentences pick out the comma that should be replaced by a semicolon:

(a) Heavy chemicals are essentially those produced in bulk and used in large quantities, fine chemicals are made on a comparatively small scale, some indeed in quantities of only a pound or two.

(b) However, technology does not make the only claim on manpower, planning, to be mentioned in a moment, also requires a comparatively high level of specialized talent.

(c) Fox Talbot's sensitive material, like Daguerre's, was silver iodide, formed not more than a day before use as a thin film on paper which was brushed successively with solutions of silver nitrate and potassium iodide, the sensitivity to light was increased by further treatment with gallic acid, the sensitizing properties of this having been discovered in 1837 by J. B. Reade, another British pioneer.

The semicolon is also used as a stronger version of the comma to mark groupings within lists, or to separate phrases that already contain commas. For example:

> And all over England towns that are historic today were as yet empty sites: Newcastle, Hull and Liverpool in the north; Boston and Kings Lynn in the east; Portsmouth and Salisbury in the south; Plymouth and Ludlow in the west. (W.G. Hoskins, *The Making of the English Landscape*, Penguin, 1970, p. 85.)

Refer to Day five if the colon in this sentence puzzles you.

Exercise 10 (revision)

Add *semicolons*, commas, full stops and capitals to this passage.

although this branch of the chemical industry is the one with which the general public most frequently comes into direct contact it is nevertheless one about which many misconceptions exist plastics are often spoken of as though there was little difference between the various kinds in fact they differ enormously in their properties plastics are often thought of as new substances in fact they have been in use for a century plastics are often regarded as cheap substitutes for other and better constructional materials such as wood metal and natural textiles in fact many have found favour on their own merits and often are far from cheap

---

Day four

Comma (*continued*)

Commas may be used to mark off a phrase or word added to a sentence that is already grammatically complete. Here are some examples:

> The construction of the new furnace, a difficult and costly operation, was completed ahead of schedule.
>
> Mr Brown, a brewery worker from Burton upon Trent, has been an Open University student for three years.
>
> Some of his hearers, however, thought he was joking.

Check that in each example the word or words between the commas could be omitted without disturbing the grammatical structure of the sentence. For example:

> The construction of the new furnace was completed ahead of schedule.

When I say that the sentence is grammatically complete without the phrase, I am not suggesting that missing out the phrase does not alter the meaning of the sentence. As you can see, this is not the case: the meaning is changed to a greater or lesser extent.

Whether or not a word like 'however' should be separated by commas (or a comma) depends on the way it is being used. The next two examples will show what I mean:

> However, hard as this theory is to understand, it will prove most useful once you have learnt it.

> However hard you try to explain it to me I am sure I shall never understand it.

Exercise 11

Add commas where appropriate:

(a) The steelworkers' representative a foundryman from Humberside argued for rapid modernization.

(b) It was his spelling not his punctuation that he needed to improve.

(c) He had no doubt a speech carefully prepared for the occasion.

(d) These incidents however trivial in themselves are liable to lead to more serious demonstrations.

Now consider this sentence:

> Having obtained planning permission, the company went ahead and built the factory.

The 'root' of this sentence is:

> The company went ahead and built the factory.

The subject of this sentence is 'the company'. The phrase 'having obtained planning permission' could equally well have been added after the subject, thus:

> The company, having obtained planning permission, went ahead and built the factory.

31

Both versions of this sentence have the same meaning. Now look at this sentence:

> The company having obtained planning permission, the objectors to the factory felt they had lost their case.

This time the 'root' is:

> The objectors to the factory felt they had lost their case.

The subject of the sentence (and of the 'root', of course) is 'the objectors to the factory'. 'The company' in this sentence is not the subject, but is a necessary part of the phrase 'the company having obtained planning permission', from which it must not be separated. A wrongly inserted comma would completely confuse the meaning:

> The company, having obtained planning permission, the objectors to the factory felt they had lost their case.

Here 'the company' looks as if it is the subject, but when the reader gets to 'the objectors' he begins to realize that the rest of the sentence does not have anything for 'the company' to be the subject of. In this example the comma after 'company' is evidently *wrong*.

Compare these two examples:

> The company went ahead and built the factory without having obtained planning permission.

> The company went ahead and built the factory, without having obtained planning permission.

Here neither sentence is wrongly punctuated. Can you see what the effect of the comma is? The first sentence is a neutral statement of the facts, but the comma in the second sentence emphasizes 'without having obtained planning permission' and implies the irregularity of the company's action.

Exercise 12

Add commas where appropriate:

(a) The fire having been lit for some time the room was quite warm.

(b) The fire having been lit for some time needed stoking.

(c) Obtaining planning permission for this factory will not be easy.

(d) The results of his early experiments being positive he was encouraged to embark on a more ambitious programme of research.

32

(e) The charge on the anode being positive attracts the negatively charged anions.

There is another session on the comma on Day six.

Exercise 13 (revision)

Add *commas*, full stops and capitals to this passage.

tyres of course have the function of spreading and cushioning the load beneath the wheels of a vehicle and in this they are extremely successful however tyres are really only one example of a whole class of blown-up structures quite apart from any cushioning effects blown-up structures provide a very effective way of evading the serious penalties in weight and cost which are incurred when we try to carry light loads over a long distance in bending or in compression

---

Day five

Colon

There is one main use of the colon: to introduce something. It may be a list of items, a statement offered as an explanation, illustration or elaboration of what has gone before, or a quotation. You will notice that I have used colons frequently in this booklet, mainly to introduce examples and exercises. Here are a few more colons:

> There are four ways in which a nucleus can alter itself: fission, alpha emission, beta emission, and gamma emission.

> Henri Becquerel also discovered the most troublesome attribute of radioactivity: its biological effects, actual and potential.

> *The Times* commented: 'The Wilberforce Report conceded almost all the miners' case'.

A particular instance of this use of the colon that you will come across frequently is where the colon introduces a series of clauses, sentences, or even paragraphs, each beginning on a new line and often numbered or lettered. In the first of the examples that follow, the colon introduces three separate sentences (questions); in the second example there is just a single sentence.

> 1.7 At the outset of the Inquiry I posed three questions which appeared to me to be sufficient to cover all issues which had then been indicated. These questions were:
>
> 1 Should oxide fuel from United Kingdom reactors be reprocessed in this country at all, whether at Windscale or elsewhere?
>
> 2 If yes, should such reprocessing be carried on at Windscale?
>
> 3 If yes, should the reprocessing plant be about double the estimated size to handle United Kingdom oxide fuels and be used, as to the spare capacity, for reprocessing foreign fuels? (*The Windscale Inquiry. Report by the Hon. Mr Justice Parker*, HMSO, 1978, pp.1–2.)
>
> 11.1 Accidents may conveniently be divided into:
>
> a accidents involving a release of radioactivity which does not escape beyond the site boundary and thus does not expose the public;
>
> b accidents which do involve a release beyond the site boundary;
>
> c accidents during transport. (*The Windscale Inquiry. Report*, p. 64.)

Notice also the use of semicolons in the last example.

Exercise 14

Add punctuation to the following:

(a) Four types of malt whisky are made in Scotland Campbeltown Highland Islay and Lowland.

(b) Time is short sixteen months is not a long time.

(c) Charles Darwin wrote 'I am convinced that Natural Selection has been the main but not exclusive means of modification.'

Exercise 15 (revision)

Add *colons*, commas, full stops and capitals to this passage.

chapman develops three basic scenarios for future patterns of fuel demand in britain 'business-as-usual' 'technical-fix' and 'low-growth' scenarios these represent respectively the virtually unrestrained projection of present trends the introduction of some technical changes to effect a more moderate growth in fuel demand and more radical proposals to effect a very definite restriction in the growth of fuel demand and aimed eventually at stabilizing demand for each case chapman explores how the various components of total fuel demand would change and the policy options that would need to be exercised to supply the various demands this exploration is succinctly conveyed but rests on considerable analysis and chapman's specialist knowledge of energy demands and the fuel industries

---

Day six

Comma (concluded)

It is not always necessary (and in some cases it is wrong) to separate a subordinate clause from the main part of a sentence, but, if the meaning of the sentence is thereby clarified, commas should be used to mark off the subordinate clause. 'Subordinate' simply means that the clause depends on another and cannot stand as a sentence on its own. In my opening sentence 'if the meaning of the sentence is thereby clarified' is a subordinate clause, and I have marked it off with commas. On the other hand, 'commas should be used to mark off the subordinate clause' is not a subordinate clause; give it a capital letter and its own full stop and it will stand on its own as a respectable sentence.

Consider the following sentences and notice how they are built up by adding successive subordinate clauses, each separated from the rest of the sentence by a comma or commas:

> The social services should receive a larger share of our national wealth.

> If the social services are to meet the increasing demands placed on them, they should receive a larger share of our national wealth.

> If, as many people have argued, the social services are to meet the increasing demands placed on them, they should receive a larger share of our national wealth.

You must consider motorways as part of a national transport system.

When you assess the needs for motorways, you must consider them as part of a national transport system.

When you assess the need for motorways, which are not as important as hospitals, you must consider them as part of a national transport system.

When you assess the need for motorways, which, when judged by these criteria, are not as important as hospitals, you must consider them as part of a national transport system.

Exercise 16

Add the necessary commas:

(a) If you are not confident about your spelling turn to the next section of this booklet where you will find some useful spelling tests and exercises.

(b) When you have studied energy in more detail as you will do later in this course you will realize how often in your everyday life you use energy-conversion devices of which the electric kettle is a familiar example.

An important point, and one that I must stress, is that if you use commas to mark off a clause in the midst of a sentence, not at the beginning or the end, you must use a pair of commas, for a single comma will hide, rather than show up, the structure of your sentence. Here is an example of such mis-use:

Commas, when used like brackets must be used in pairs.

It should, of course, be:

Commas, when used like brackets, must be used in pairs.

Look back at the sentence above that begins, 'An important point ...'; towards the end of that sentence I inserted 'rather than show up' into the clause, 'for a single comma will hide the structure of your sentence', thus:

... you must use a pair of commas, for a single comma will hide, rather than show up, the structure of your sentence.

But watch what happens when I am careless and miss out the comma after 'rather than show up':

36

... you must use a pair of commas, for a single comma will hide, rather than show up the structure of your sentence.

Now the single comma appears to be bashful and hides itself, not 'the structure of your sentence'.

There is one use of the comma with subordinate clauses that seems to cause difficulties even for experienced writers. Look at these two sentences:

John admired the car which was in the garage.

John admired the car, which was in the garage.

You can see how the comma alters the meaning. In the first sentence the clause 'which was in the garage' tells us *which* car it was that John admired; we can call this a 'defining' clause. In the second sentence 'which was in the garage' is an additional piece of information about a particular car that, presumably, has already been identified. This we can call a 'describing' or 'commenting' clause. It may help you to sort out 'defining' and 'describing' clauses if you remember that *which* can be replaced by *that* in a 'defining' clause, but not in a 'describing' clause. For example,

John admired the car that was in the garage.

'Defining' and 'describing' clauses may also begin with such words as *who, whose, where* and *when*. Here are some examples:

Defining:

The engineer who built the Menai Bridge was Thomas Telford, a man whose work I much admire.

You should do that on a day when there is no wind.

Show me the site where the power station is to be built.

Describing:

Thomas Telford, who was first President of the Institute of Civil Engineers, was without doubt a great engineer.

You can do it on Saturday, when you do not have to go to work.

Exercise 17

See if you can pick out the 'defining' and 'describing' clauses in these sentences:

(a) I became aware that my pursuer, who by now was only a few yards off, was the man whom I had seen that morning at the inn.

(b) Last summer I went back to the town where I was born.

(c) That was in the days when beer was twopence a pint.

(d) My next trip is to Sheffield, where we are opening a new factory.

Exercise 18

Pick out the wrongly punctuated sentences and correct them. Also identify the 'defining' and 'describing' clauses:

(a) People, who live in country districts, are particularly affected by the withdrawal of bus services.

(b) I want you to know the basic rules, which govern punctuation.

(c) In this book he gives a very balanced account of nuclear power which I think you should read.

(d) It was a letter from my mother who was worried because I had not written lately.

(e) Usually my brother met me at the station, but on that memorable Friday it was my father who came to meet me.

Exercise 19 (revision)

Add *commas*, a semicolon, full stops and capitals to this passage.

although bats flourish and survive very well today pterodactyls were superseded by birds which have feathers a great many years ago it is possible of course that the extinction of pterodactyls had nothing to do with structural considerations but it is also possible that there is something special about feathers which gives birds an edge over other flying creatures when i worked at the royal aircraft establishment i used to ask my superiors from time to time whether it would not perhaps be better if aeroplanes had feathers but i seldom succeeded in extracting a rational or even a patient answer to this question

---

Here are two final points about commas:

1   When writing your essays try to be generous in your use of full stops and sparing in your use of commas. You will find that several shorter sentences separated by full stops provide a more effective means of communicating your ideas than one long sentence full of commas.

2   After writing an essay you should always read over it. If you find a sentence that is ambiguous or does not say quite what you intended, *do not add commas* in an attempt to clarify the meaning. Re-cast the sentence or even break it down into shorter ones.

Day seven

Apostrophe

1   The apostrophe is used to indicate possession of a thing or quality by someone or some thing:

Thing possessed		*Possessor*	*Form using apostrophe*
the boundary	of	the system	the system's boundary
the components	of	the system	the system's components
the drawings	of	the architect	the architect's drawings
the drawings	of	the architects	the architects' drawings
the drawings	of	the children	the children's drawings
the charter	of	the university	the university's charter
the aims	of	the course	the course's aims
the aperture	of	the lens	the lens's aperture
the apertures	of	the lenses	the lenses' apertures

You can always make a possessive form of a singular word by adding 's, but in some cases it is not a good idea. For example, you would not write *the synthesis's simplicity* for *the simplicity of the synthesis*.

The possessive form of plural words sometimes causes difficulty. If the word forms its plural regularly, by adding -s or -es, then the possessive form has just an apostrophe after the s: *architects', lenses'. Children,* however, is the plural of *child* and forms its possessive by adding 's: *children's.* Other plural possessive forms in 's include *men's* and *women's. People* is an interesting case. It is often treated as a plural, although of course it has a plural of its own (*peoples*). This seems to cause confusion about the form of the possessive. The possessive of *people* is *people's.*

Try not to confuse the process of forming a possessive with that of forming a plural. For example, you know that *university* has *universities* as its plural, but do not let that mislead you into thinking that in the possessive form the -y has to be replaced by -ie before you add 's. You simply add 's to university: *university's.*

Exercise 20

Rewrite these phrases using apostrophes:

(a) the gain of the amplifier

(b) the gains of the amplifiers

(c) the importance of chemistry

(d) the properties of the gas

(e) the properties of the gases

(f) the occupations of the men

---

2   An apostrophe is used to show where some letter or letters have been missed out:

it's	it is	don't	do not
you'll	you will	they're	they are
he's	he is (*or* he has)		

Apostrophes are only used in this way to represent direct speech or when writing in a 'conversational' style. There is probably little use for them in an essay.

The apostrophe is similarly used to show where figures have been missed out, especially in dates:

a '59 Morris Minor
I haven't been there since '72.

3   Apostrophes are *not* used to form plurals of initials, abbreviations or figures.

The plural of MP, for example, is MPs, that of e.m.f. is e.m.f.s, and *sixes and sevens* is written with figures as *6s and 7s*. Initials like MP, BBC or OU form possessives in the regular way. Here is an example:

The BBC's response to the MPs' criticisms was to invite the MPs to take part in a discussion programme on broadcasting in the 1980s.

4   It's and its

It's easy to confuse these two, perhaps because they each seem deceptively simple.

40

It's means *it is* (the apostrophe indicating that a letter has been left out):

It's a long way to Tipperary.

Its denotes possession:

The car had its front wheels in the ditch.

Exercise 21

Fill in the blanks with *it's* or *its*:

(a) _____ roof was insulated.

(b) _____ too early for the pubs to be open.

(c) I must have overloaded _____ circuits.

(d) _____ main disadvantage is _____ weight.

(e) _____ the latest model and _____ performance is second to none.

(f) _____ not easy to understand relativity theory because _____ concepts are mathematical.

Exercise 22 (revision)

Add *apostrophes*, a colon, commas, full stops and capitals to this passage.

why have i called the package a 'unit'? because it represents a weeks worth of your time one week of student study is the basic unit of the open universitys arithmetic the remainder of this course is built around a set of 'blocks' each of which contains several units worth of work studying each unit will involve not just reading text but also watching television listening to radio working through audiovision and answering assignments

---

Day eight

Brackets (*parentheses*)

Brackets (parentheses) are used to insert an additional piece of information into a sentence that is already complete. They are particularly helpful if you wish to refer your reader to a diagram, a table, another page of your essay, or a reference in another place:

> Initially the simple sugar, glucose (Figure 1), is synthesized in leaves by the action of sunlight.
>
> The Young's modulus varies very much according to the kind of chemical substance we are dealing with (see Table 2).
>
> Kochhar suggests (*Nature*, vol. 277, p. 116) that this is what happened in the precursor of the Crab system.

You may also find brackets useful for introducing an abbreviation that you intend to use later:

> On 24 August last year Professor Henry Bedson wrote to the World Health Organization (WHO) to reply to criticisms that his smallpox laboratory did not come up to WHO's safety standards. (*New Scientist*, 4 January 1979, p. 8.)

Brackets are also used for expressing quantities in an alternative way or for adding dates:

> It will be a mild afternoon, with temperatures rising to 15 °C (60 °F).
>
> A masonry arch can span 200 feet (60 metres) or so without much difficulty.
>
> Let us begin at the beginning with Newton (1642–1727), who said that action and reaction are equal and opposite.

Where brackets are used in a sentence at the point where another punctuation mark is needed (e.g. the comma in the last example), the other punctuation mark follows the closing bracket but it must not be left out.

Use brackets sparingly, and make sure that the information contained in them is brief and to the point. Do not use them in an essay for chatty little asides or niggling qualifications; nor should points that forward your argument be placed in brackets. Here is a bad example:

> Among the advantages cited in favour of the 'pricing' approach are claims that it would be administratively cheaper to operate, that it would be fairer (because it would leave decisions with the

people who know what's economically and commercially possible), and that it would be more flexible (because it would be relatively simple to increase 'prices' for pollutants which were giving rise to special concern).

Exercise 23

Add brackets and commas to this passage:

'Polychlorinated biphenyls PCBs should be regarded as if they were carcinogenic to humans' says a report by the International Agency for Research on Cancer *IARC Monographs*, vol. 18. But the authoritative and cautious IARC says there is insufficient evidence to decide whether polybrominated biphenyls PBBs the close chemical cousins of PCBs are also carcinogenic.

You will be introduced to the uses of brackets in mathematics in the *Numeracy* tributaries. As you will see there, brackets do quite a different job in mathematics and the rules for using them are therefore different. When using brackets non-mathematically, avoid 'nesting' of brackets. By 'nesting' I mean this sort of thing:

> The total area required works out at 17 hectares. (One hectare equals about $2\frac{1}{2}$ acres (see Appendix).)

One way to avoid this here would be to use a dash to separate the inner parenthesis:

> The total area required works out at 17 hectares. (One hectare equals about $2\frac{1}{2}$ acres – see Appendix.)

Exercise 24 (revision)

Add *brackets* (*parentheses*), commas, full stops and capitals to this passage.

figure 16 shows the pattern of energy flow in the united kingdom in 1975 gross consumption of *primary energy* in the united kingdom was approximately 2425 TWh 1 TWh = 10^9 kWh but because of inefficiencies in energy conversion and distribution some 30 per cent or so 725 TWh is lost between producer and consumer even when this *delivered energy* finally arrives at the point of consumption further losses of around 30 per cent 725 TWh occur in the appliances and processes in which it is used central-heating boilers for instance have efficiencies of only 60 per cent

or so open coal fires are even worse with a typical efficiency of only .
20 per cent and motor cars with internal combustion engines are still less
efficient less than 20 per cent

An aside on square brackets

The brackets I have been discussing so far are known to printers as
parentheses. Square brackets [ ] are what a printer would call 'brackets'.
In your own writing you will probably not need to use square brackets
(except, perhaps, in writing mathematics), but you will come across them
in your reading, so I shall explain their use. Square brackets are used by
editors to indicate a comment or explanation that has been added to a
quoted passage, or an alteration from the original. As an illustration, look
back at the quotation from the *New Scientist* of 4 January 1979 near
the beginning of Day eight. It is printed there just as it appeared in the
original, but, if the object had been to help you identify the event more
precisely, the quotation might have been presented like this:

> On 24 August [1978] Professor Henry Bedson wrote to the
> World Health Organization (WHO) to reply to criticisms that
> his smallpox laboratory [at the Medical School of Birmingham
> University] did not come up to WHO's safety standards.

Day nine

Hyphen

The prime function of the hyphen is to prevent ambiguity. Its main use is
to link the parts of compound words:

> mother-in-law, bench-mark, cross-section, fall-out, frying-pan,
> test-tube, wing-span.

Hyphens occur in numbers, when they are written out in full:

> fifty-seven, nine-tenths, one hundred and forty-four, six and
> seven-eighths.

The hyphen is used to form compound adjectives:

> high-rise flats, a water-cooled engine, a ten-storey office block,
> long-term planning, twentieth-century technology.

Notice that the need for a hyphen will depend on the way a phrase is used:

His friend lived near by.	He went into a near-by pub.
That performance was first class.	That was a first-class performance.
Use a little common sense.	He has a common-sense approach to economics.
There must be a short circuit somewhere.	You cannot short-circuit it without blowing the fuse.
Your subscriptions are not up to date.	Have you got an up-to-date timetable?

Exercise 25

Add hyphens to the following, where appropriate:

(a) The start of the second phase of the three year programme was set back a month.

(b) This will be a set back for your far fetched schemes; perhaps it will bring you down to earth.

(c) This recently published report contains up to date information on low level radiation leaks from advanced gas cooled reactors.

A hyphen is sometimes needed with a prefix. The following examples illustrate some of the cases that require a hyphen. In many cases you will need to refer to your dictionary for help.

(a) To avoid a doubled letter or other combination that might be misread:

re-erect,	but	rebuild;
pre-existing,	but	preoccupied;
sub-basement,	but	subcontinent;
co-author,	but	cosine.

(b) With re-, to indicate that it is being added to something that is being done again, rather than forming part of a well-known compound word. For example:

The ladies' darts team has been re-formed.

Other examples are: re-cover, re-create.

(c) Again with re-, the hyphen is used to emphasize the idea of repetition. Compare these two sentences:

> You may need to redraw your rough sketches before sending them with your assignment.

> I have drawn and re-drawn this diagram, but I cannot get it right.

(d) Finally, less-familiar words formed with a prefix may need a hyphen, whereas a well-established word will not. Again, you will find your dictionary of great help. Here are a couple of examples:

> pre-scientific, but prehistoric;
> ultra-careful, but ultraviolet light.

Exercise 26 (revision)

Add punctuation (capitals, commas, a colon, full stops, brackets – or parentheses – and *hyphens*) to this passage:

on the other hand the *unit* costs or 'run on costs' of printing the magazine on a hand operated duplicating machine will be relatively high for various reasons

a the machine because it is hand operated can produce relatively few copies per hour so the labour cost of each copy is relatively high

b the machine for technical reasons has to use fairly heavy paper which makes the cost of each copy relatively high also the stencil being made of waxed paper will break up after say a thousand copies or so and a new one will have to be typed

c the machine prints only one page at a time so that when all the sheets thirty two of them for a sixty four page magazine are finally printed it takes a long time to collate them by hand and staple them into a magazine

---

Day ten

Dash

It's tempting to use the dash as an all-purpose punctuation mark. Avoid this temptation. Lots of dashes are often a symptom of poorly structured writing. If you find you are sprinkling dashes on the page, ask yourself whether your sentence construction is under control. You can write good, well-punctuated English without using dashes at all, but they do have accepted uses.

1   In pairs, to mark a parenthesis:

> (a) No one has yet built a living organism – however simple – starting from scratch.

> (b) A combination of three types of study – two on humans and one on animals – indicates strongly that alcohol is harmful to unborn babies.

In this use a pair of dashes acts as a 'weak' pair of brackets, and a pair of commas would separate the parenthesis even more weakly.

Exercise 27

Rewrite the above examples using brackets and then commas in place of the dashes. Try to decide for each sentence which punctuation best fits the sense.

---

2   To introduce an explanation or development of the point that comes immediately before:

> (a) The Chinese are thrifty people – the earth dug out was used to make bricks for the tunnel walls.

> (b) Already it has sold six systems – three in Denmark, two in Spain and one in Italy.

Here the dash is being used rather like a colon.

Exercise 28

Replace the dashes in the above examples with colons. Do you think this an improvement?

Exercise 29

Look at the following passage and try to decide what is the function of each dash. Then try to replace the dashes with other punctuation marks.

A purely inorganic compound with optical activity – the first for almost 50 years – has just been synthesized by Robert Gillard and Franz Winmer of University College, Cardiff. Most known optically active compounds – molecules with structures that cannot be superimposed upon their mirror images – contain carbon atoms. They are either organic compounds, or chelates – complexes of transition metals where the carbon atoms help form the claw-like ligands. (*New Scientist*, 11 January 1979, p. 92.)

There are some other uses for dashes in printed text. These need not concern you when you do your own writing, for in manuscript or when typed they will look the same as hyphens. However, as you will come across them in your reading, I shall try to explain these uses simply.

3   To indicate a link or non-grammatical relation between two words. Here are some examples of what I mean:

> parent–teacher association;   cost–benefit analysis
>
> The main axis lies in a north–south direction.
>
> Near the village of Watford in Northamptonshire the London–Yorkshire motorway (the M1) and the main London–Glasgow railway line run alongside each other for two or three miles.
>
> Classical 'wet' chemical analyses include gravimetric methods, acid–base titrations and oxidation–reduction reactions.
>
> For a nuclear reaction the separate conservation laws for mass and energy are replaced by a single law of conservation of mass–energy.
>
> The Heisenberg uncertainty principle arises from the dual particle–wave nature of matter.

4   To indicate a range of values or the extent of a period:

> Stainless steel contains 70–90 per cent iron, 12–20 per cent chromium and 0.1–0.7 per cent carbon.
>
> Telford (1757–1834) – the 'Colossus of roads', or 'Pontifex Maximus', as Southey called him – probably built more bridges than anyone else in history.
>
> The best times for sowing a lawn are September–October or mid-March–mid-April.

5   Where something is named jointly after two people:

> In the open-hearth, or Siemens–Martin, process steel is made by melting roughly equal quantities of pig-iron and scrap steel with some iron ore.
>
> The Geiger–Müller tube will detect any type of ionizing particle or radiation.

Exercise 30 (revision)

Add punctuation to the following:

(a) it is found that meteors fall into two distinct classes the stony and the iron nickel types with a few intermediate or stony iron types

(b) the beer lambert law is an extension of a law proposed by lambert in 1760 which stated that layers of equal thickness of a homogeneous material absorb equal proportions of light

(c) einstein suggested that the path of a particle in four dimensional space time is a geodesic

Spelling

Day one

It is well known that English is a difficult language to spell correctly, for quite often the words are not pronounced in a way that makes the spelling clear. Most people do spell most words correctly, but there are many words that are commonly misspelt. It is these we shall be dealing with over the next six days.

If you already know you are poor at spelling or you try these exercises and find unfamiliar words that you have difficulty with, get a dictionary, keep it handy and refer to it constantly. As you will see, there are few rules for spelling. The best way to learn how to spell is to check with a dictionary and then to test yourself repeatedly until you are so familiar with a word that you are sure of its spelling.

Double letters

It is generally clear from the sound of a word whether or not a vowel, that is, *a, e, i, o* or *u*, should be doubled (compare *red* and *reed*, or *hot* and *hoot*) and it is only *e* and *o* that are commonly doubled. Doubling a consonant, in other words a letter that is not a vowel, doesn't have such an obvious effect on pronunciation; as a result it is easy to be confused about when to double consonants.

Particularly, when adding *-ing* or *-ed* to the end of verbs, that is, 'doing' or 'being' words, it is difficult to know whether or not to double a single consonant at the end of the simple verb. For example, does *drop* become *droping* or *dropping*, *droped* or *dropped*? Here *dropping* and *dropped* are correct; the *p* is doubled. But what happens to the *p* in *droop* and *drape*? In both these verbs the *p* is not doubled. The correct forms are *drooping* and *drooped*, and *draping* and *draped*.

For words like these there is a simple general rule, which you may find helpful, although there are some exceptions. The rule is:

> Double a single final consonant if the word is pronounced as a short sound (e.g. *drop*), but do not double the final consonant if the word is pronounced as a long sound (e.g. *droop, drape*).

Here are a few more examples:

> *Short sound*
> get, getting;   win, winning;   mat, matting, matted

51

Long sound
gain, gaining, gained;   meet, meeting;   state, stating, stated

The same rule can also be used for adjectives, that is, 'describing' words, when writing the forms that end with *-er* and *-est*. For example:

hot, hotter, hottest
sweet, sweeter, sweetest
white, whiter, whitest

It is usually longer words that cause problems. For longer verbs there is another rule, which also relates to the way the word is spoken:

Double a single final consonant if the stress falls at the end of the word, but do not double the final consonant if the stress falls elsewhere.

Here are a couple of examples where the stress falls at the end of the word and the final consonant is doubled:

omit, omitting, omitted
infer, inferring, inferred

In the next examples, the stress falls at the beginning of the word and the final consonant is not doubled:

bias, biasing, biased
focus, focusing, focused
offer, offering, offered
visit, visiting, visited

A notable exception to this rule is that in English (as opposed to American) usage almost all verbs ending with a single *-l* double the final *-l*:

travel, travelling, travelled
model, modelling, modelled

The only really safe rule, of course, is: *Look it up in your dictionary.*

Exercise 31

Complete these sentences by adding the correct ending in the blanks.

(a) Please begin at the begin_____.

(b) The council has allot_____ a larger proportion of its budget to technical education.

(c) History will show how much we have benefit_____ from the silicon chip.

(d) His argument was so compel_____ that we all ended by agreeing with him.

Some words have double consonants that follow no rule and can only be learnt through practice.

Exercise 32

Here is a list of ten words, three of which are spelt correctly. The others should have doubled consonants which have not been doubled here. First, identify the correct words, then rewrite correctly those that are incorrect. When you have finished check with your dictionary.

Word	*Right/wrong*	*Correct spelling*
(a) sucesful		
(b) acoustic		
(c) ocasionaly		
(d) comitee		
(e) exagerate		
(f) abreviate		
(g) paralel		
(h) omision		
(i) procedure		
(j) develop		

Day two

ei *and* ie

As a child you probably learnt some such jingle as '*i* before *e* except after *c*, when the sound is *ee*'. Of course, there are exceptions (e.g. *seize*) and you may have felt that the rule is not very helpful.

Exercise 33

Choose the correct spelling in each sentence.

(a) He acheived/achieved success through hard work.

(b) A quotient/quoteint is the number obtained when one number is divided by another.

(c) The workmanship was so deficeint/deficient that the council refused to accept the property.

(d) Black beams in the cieling/ceiling gave the room an atmosphere of age.

(e) The way we percieve/perceive ourselves affects our relations with other people.

-er *and* -or

Both -*er* and -*or* endings are found in words that describe people in terms of what they do or what their occupation is, for example,

> actor, tailor, decorator, collector, donor;
> painter, butcher, reader, angler, gardener.

The ending -*or* is found in words for *things* that do something, for example,

> generator, motor, incinerator, radiator,

but watch out for exceptions such as computer and propeller.

Exercise 34

Decide which of these words are spelt correctly, give the correct spelling for the others and check with your dictionary before looking at the answers.

Word	*Right/Wrong*	*Correct spelling*
(a) consumer		
(b) accelerater		
(c) manufacturer		

54

Word	Right/Wrong	Correct spelling

(d) inventer

(e) distributer

(f) designer

Day three

-ant *and* -ent; -ance (-ancy) *and* -ence (-ency)

There is no reliable way of telling if a word ends in -*ant* or -*ent* because the sounds of these endings are not clearly distinguished. However, if the word ends with -*ent* in one form, the other form will end with -*ence* or -*ency*. For example,

> frequent,   frequency
> intelligent, intelligence

If the ending is -*ant*, the related ending is -*ance* or -*ancy*, for example,

> important, importance
> tolerant,   tolerance
> infant,   infancy

Exercise 35

Complete these sentences by adding the missing letters to the words.

(a) All chemical elements and compounds are subst_____s, but solutions are mixtures.

(b) If there had been any recurr_____ of the events, the club would have been closed.

(c) The infer_____s drawn from the market research data proved correct.

(d) The properties and dimensions of a piece of material determine its electrical resist_____.

(e) It is too soon to evaluate the perform_____ of the new equipment.

-ious, -ous *and* -eous

The endings *-ious*, *-ous* and *-eous* are all used to make adjectives and they are often confused. The pair *-ious* and *-eous* cause the most problems because they sound the same. For example, listen to the sounds of these pairs of words:

conscious, gaseous;   courteous, dubious.

There are no rules for these endings and the correct endings must be learnt.

Exercise 36

Add the correct ending to each of these words. Their meanings are in brackets to avoid any confusion.

(a) homogen_____   (composed of similar constituents)

(b) nutrit_____   (nourishing)

(c) precar_____   (uncertain, risky)

(d) meticul_____   (over-exact, punctilious)

(e) numer_____   (very many)

(f) erron_____   (wrong)

(g) caut_____   (careful)

(h) enorm_____   (huge)

-able *and* -ible

Adjectives can be formed from verbs by adding an *-able* or an *-ible* ending. For example,

accept,   acceptable
advise,   advisable
digest,   digestible
reverse,   reversible

There are many rules for deciding which ending a word should have.

Here is the simplest, but, as you can see, it doesn't cover every occasion.

> If the part of the word before the ending is a complete word (perhaps with a dropped final *e*), the end is probably *-able*; for example,
>
> > love, lovable
> > tax, taxable
>
> If the part of the word before the ending is not a complete word, the ending is probably *-ible*; for example,
>
> > horrible, edible

(Note that *digestible* and *reversible* are exceptions to this rule.)

Exercise 37

Choose the correctly spelt word from those offered in each sentence. Remember to check with your dictionary.

(a) Fine food and agreeable/agreeible/agreable company combine for the most pleasant evenings.

(b) Haste is no excuse for illegable/illegible writing.

(c) As the fog cleared the ship was just visable/visible on the horizon.

(d) Children's toys should be made of durable/durible materials for hard use.

(e) The system is flexable/flexible enough to allow for production delays.

(f) All cars must be fitted with adjustable/adjustible seat belts.

Day five

-ary *and* -ery

Here is a useful guide, although it is not a rigid rule.

> Words ending in *-ery* are usually nouns, that is 'naming' words, and contain a complete smaller word within them, for example,

noun	smaller word
confectionery	confection
discovery	discover
stationery	stationer

Words ending in -*ary* are usually adjectives, for example,
documentary, tributary, stationary

However, note exceptions such as library.

Exercise 38

Examine this list of words and decide in each case whether the missing
letter is *e* or *a*; then write the correct spelling in the space provided.

(a) bin_ry   _____

(b) machin_ry   _____

(c) necess_ry   _____

(d) contempor_ry   _____

(e) periph_ry   _____

(f) deliv_ry   _____

(g) prim_ry   _____

Have you checked your answers with your dictionary?

-sion *and* -tion

Words ending in -*tion* and -*sion* are usually nouns formed from verbs,
and some guidance about which ending to use can be obtained by
studying the ending of the verb from which the noun is formed.

A noun ending in -*sion* is formed from verbs ending in:

-*nd*   (expand, expansion)
-*de*   (provide, provision)
-*ss*   (discuss, discussion)
-*mit*   (omit, omission)
-*pel*   (propel, propulsion – note the *u*)
-*vert*   (divert, diversion)

A noun ending in -*tion* is formed from verbs ending in:

-*ct*   (act, action)
-*te*   (create, creation)
-*pose*   (dispose, disposition)

Exercise 39

Make nouns with *-sion* or *-tion* endings from the following words:

(a) extend   _____   (d) transmit   _____

(b) distribute   _____   (e) restrict   _____

(c) repulse   _____   (f) construct   _____

Day six

-ceed, -cede *and* -sede

Words containing these endings cause confusion, because there is no rule for their spelling. Words ending in *-ceed* and *-cede* come from the same Latin stem, meaning to go or to yield, and have simply changed spelling through time. Supersede is the only word in English to end in *-sede*.

exceed	accede	supersede
proceed	concede	
succeed	intercede	
	precede	
	recede	
	secede	

Exercise 40

A list of dictionary meanings is given. Write the correct word from the above lists next to the meaning, then check in your own dictionary.

(a) to go on, or continue   _____

(b) to replace   _____

(c) to go before   _____

(d) to turn out well   _____

Exercise 41

Here are a few more words people sometimes have problems with.
Choose the correct spelling and write it at the side. Then check with your
dictionary.

(a) asertain/assertain/ascertain   _____

(b) miscellaneous/miscelaneous/miscelanous   _____

(c) consious/consciouse/conscious   _____

(d) disciplin/disipline/discipline   _____

(e) artificial/artifisial/artifitial   _____

(f) oficial/ofitial/official   _____

(g) escential/essential/esential   _____

(h) inisial/initial/inishal   _____

Remember that the fact that you have a problem with a word could be
because it is an exception to a rule, so the golden rule is:

Use your dictionary.

Grammar

Day one

Sentence structure

Most sentences contain a subject and an associated verb, that is, a 'being' or 'doing' word. The subject is the person or thing that is doing the doing or being. Here is an example of a complete sentence:

> In the summer of 1977 Jones made his last appearance before a TGWU convention.

'Jones' is the subject of the sentence. 'Made' is the verb.

If I wanted to add further information to this sentence, I could do it in either of two ways. I could add a few words of description in a phrase:

> In the summer of 1977 Jones made his last appearance before a TGWU convention, pleading for a third year of wage restraint.

The other way is for me to construct two short sentences, each with its own subject and verb:

> In the summer of 1977 *Jones made* his last appearance before a TGWU convention. *He pleaded* for a third year of wage restraint.

If you think that your sentences seem long and clumsy, break them into shorter sentences, but always make sure that each one contains a main subject and verb.

Exceptions to sentences containing a subject and verb are generally used to achieve a particular effect, as in slogans and commands. When writing your assignments, essays and study notes you are not in the business of giving commands, nor are slogans appropriate.

Exercise 42

Which of these examples are complete sentences? For each complete sentence state the subject and its associated verb. Rewrite the non-sentences. (Your rewritten sentences may differ from those in the answer section, but try to check that there is a main subject and a main verb each time.)

(a) The related concepts of force and inertia in physics.

(b) Worms and insects which survive in the soil.

(c) More than a hundred years ago, John Stuart Mill realized that industrial society, by its very nature, could not last for long and that the stable society that must replace it would be far better.

(d) From the statement that the whole is greater than the sum of its parts it follows that the parts are simpler than the whole.

(e) A natural cycle for every element needed for life, each with its own natural circulation rate.

(f) Pollution from getting rid of wastes at the least possible cost.

(g) Gaseous emissions may well become a significant problem as breeder reactors and fuel reprocessing plant come into operation.

(h) Generating electric currents from mechanical motion and hence of converting mechanical energy to electrical.

(i) The rate of man's technological advancement has always been determined by his discovery and manipulation of materials to meet his needs.

(j) The process of cracking, by which large molecules are broken down into smaller ones by means of high temperatures and pressures.

(k) Soil deterioration and eventually erosion by intensification of farming.

(l) Although it is true to say that maintenance, wear and tear and petrol costs are fairly closely related to the time spent travelling, it seems that many motorists make decisions about a journey on the basis of average petrol costs per mile.

Day two

Prepositions

A preposition is a word placed usually before a noun or its equivalent. Examples of prepositions are:

> in, over, across, with, for, upon

These are useful little words that help to show the relations between other words. For example,

> to have an affinity with
> to be contingent upon

English is particularly rich in prepositions. Judiciously used, they help us to give our thoughts precise expression. Make sure you use the correct preposition. Here are some examples of incorrect use of prepositions, followed by the right ones:

It seemed *like* the whole country was on holiday.	(incorrect)
It seemed *as if* the whole country was on holiday.	(correct)
I am different *than* my sister.	(incorrect)
I am different *from* my sister.	(correct)
I have been suffering *with* bronchitis this winter.	(incorrect)
I have been suffering *from* bronchitis this winter.	(correct)

Exercise 43

What is wrong with each of these sentences? Write the correct sentences in the spaces provided.

(a) Stainless steel consists in carbon steel with nickel and chromium added.

(b) I had scarcely begun the calculations than my calculator batteries went flat.

(c) Will you join me in a pint?

(d) The strike was called to protest at the low bonus offered.

(e) All applicants will be judged on their knowledge of management techniques.

Pronouns

My brother and me or *More about getting the grammar right*

Confusion over pronouns (e.g. me, him, it, you) often occurs. Most of us were told as children not to say, 'you and me', when we meant, 'you and I'. This often results in people writing, 'you and I', when they should write, 'you and me'. One does not say, 'He gave it to I' (except in the remoter parts of Somerset); one says, 'He gave it to me', and yet you might hesitate about saying, 'He gave it to my brother and me'. *This, however, is correct.*

The best way, therefore, to decide whether you should write *I* or *me*, *he* or *him*, *she* or *her*, *they* or *them*, when there are other people in the sentence, is to imagine the sentence with the other people left out (if that is possible).

Exercise 44

Correct these sentences where necessary:

(a) He is afraid of George and I.

(b) George and I are afraid of him and her.

(c) He gave it to both me and he.

(d) Between you and I, he probably won't come.

(e) A quarrel arose between him and me.

A note on 'like'

> I cannot recall all the formulae like I used to.

In this sentence the word 'like' is being used as a joining word. In spoken English it is frequently used in this way, but it is not correct, either in written or spoken English. The sentence should be either:

> I cannot recall all the formulae as I used to.

or

> I cannot recall all the formulae in the way (that) I used to.

If it helps, try to associate:

like with a noun (like somebody, something), for example,

> Nothing succeeds like success.

as with a verb (in a similar manner, way), for example,

> Nothing succeeds as success does.

Day three

Agreement of subject and verb

You saw in the examples and exercises in Day one that the main subject and its associated verb often become separated from each other. They should always agree in number, that is to say, a singular subject takes a singular verb and a plural subject takes a plural verb.

Look at the following sentences. Which are the main subjects and verbs in them? Does the verb agree in number with its subject?

> The strength and ductility of a solid depends on how easily cracks will occur.

> The presence of such substances as carbon, silicon and sulphur affect the behaviour of cast iron.

In the first example there is a double subject, 'strength and ductility', and a plural form of the verb is required (*depend*).

In the second sentence the subject of the sentence is 'presence' and therefore a singular form of the verb is required (*affects*).

When you are using the verb 'to be' (I am, you are, etc.), if the subject before it has a number the verb agrees with that subject, otherwise it agrees with the number of the subject associated with it but which comes after it.

Here are some sentences to illustrate this point:

> In the mid-nineteenth century, included among particularly unhealthy trades, there *was* the Midlands hardware *industry* centred around Birmingham.
>
> In the mid-nineteenth century, included among particularly unhealthy trades, there *were* the Midlands hardware *factories*.
>
> In the mid-nineteenth century, the Midlands hardware *industry was* one of the particularly unhealthy trades.

Exercise 45

Correct the following sentences:

(a) The amount of viscosity exhibited by different fluids vary.

(b) So much water and oil has been drawn from underground that the resources are much depleted.

(c) A library of subroutines contribute to the value of a computer installation in much the same way as an extra piece of equipment would do.

(d) The limitation of exhaust emissions and atmospheric pollution generally by the application of smoke control regulations are a further step in the improvement of the road-user's environment.

(e) The dotted curves in the figure show the distribution of population in the previous ten years.

Doubling prepositions

It is common for people to add unnecessary prepositions. Here are some examples:

> Our theatre seats were very near to the orchestra.

In this example *near* is enough on its own, *to* should be left out:

> Our theatre seats were very near the orchestra.
>
> We always help old ladies off of the bus.   (*Of* is unnecessary.)

We spent most of our holidays inside of the caravan.   (*Of* is unnecessary.)

Prepositions are sometimes added unnecessarily to verbs:

The fuel tank was emptied out.   (*Out* is implied in *emptied*.)

In *Living with Technology* you will be studying about the effects of technology on your own life.   (*About* is unnecessary.)

Connect the inlet pipe up with the tap.   (*Up* is unnecessary.)

In these examples the extra preposition is redundant, and should be omitted.

Exercise 46

What is wrong with each of these sentences? For each sentence mark the unnecessary word.

(a) Ever since the oil crisis the cost of food has risen steadily.

(b) She suffered a broken leg when she was knocked off of her bike.

(c) Being as this tutorial will finish so late, there'll be no time for a drink.

(d) There were approximately about ten per cent more students this year.

(e) It took three days by air to reach Australia up until Concorde flew that route.

Day four

Ending sentences

Do not use a preposition to end a sentence with.

Do you agree with this advice?

There is probably no need to point out that the sentence itself breaks its own rule. A better version is:

Do not end a sentence with a preposition.

Sir Ernest Gowers advises, 'Do not hesitate to end a sentence with a preposition if your ear tells you that that is where the preposition goes best.' (*The Complete Plain Words*, p. 185.) In some sentences it is almost impossible not to end with a preposition. For example,

> His head should be cut off.
>
> Look at what you're standing on.
>
> Tell me what you're frightened of.

Exercise 47

Rewrite the following sentences so that the preposition does not occur at the end.

(a) What have you given it to me for?

(b) It was their new house that I was envious of.

(c) When I began the journey, I was unsure where I was going to.

Affect and effect

Affect is mainly used as a verb, and in two senses. In the one sense 'to affect' means 'to influence', for example,

> I don't suppose microprocessors will *affect* my style of living.

In the second sense, 'to affect' means 'to make a show or pretence of', for example,

> I *affected* an air of indifference to the whole matter.

Effect can be used either as a verb or as a noun. As a verb it means 'to cause something to happen', 'to bring about something', for example,

> He used a safety pin and a piece of elastic to effect a temporary repair.

Here is an example of its use as a noun:

> The effect of microprocessors at work will be to increase the speed with which we deal with correspondence.

Exercise 48

Fill in the gaps in these sentences, using parts of either *affect* or *effect*.

(a) He _____ to be unmoved by the team's criticism.

(b) These measures are designed to _____ the motorist.

(c) The _____ of these measures will be to aid the motorist.

(d) The replacement of the valve was _____ quietly and smoothly.

In the following sentence both affect and effect make sense, but the meanings are different.

> Extra training may affect his promotion.

This means that the training may influence his promotion.

> Extra training may effect his promotion.

Here the meaning is that training may bring about his promotion.

Exercise 49

Explain the difference in meaning between these two sentences.

(a) A further adjustment in the position of the equipment will affect its quiet running.

(b) A further adjustment in the position of the equipment will effect its quiet running.

Day five

Singulars, plurals and collective nouns

There are many words that denote a collection of things or people but which are singular in form, for example, *team, herd, committee, council, government, Parliament*. These are known as collective nouns. You can follow a collective noun with either a singular or plural verb, depending on whether you are thinking of the collection individually or all together. For example, you may write either:

> The Government has decided to ration petrol.

or   The Government have decided to ration petrol.

Both sentences are correct.

However, when other words in the sentence, apart from the verb, refer to the collective noun you must be consistent:

> (a) The Government *has* decided that *they* will ration petrol.

> (b) The Government *have* decided that *they* will ration petrol.

> (c) The Government *has* decided that *it* will ration petrol.

(a) is incorrect; (b) and (c) are correct.

As a general rule the following words are used with a singular verb: *neither, each, either, every*. Here are some examples of correct usage:

> In the case of particles in a closed container, *each exerts* a small impulse when it collides with the walls of the container.

> *Either* physical or mathematical modelling *is used* to illustrate the behaviour of the system.

Note. You may write 'none *is*' or 'none *are*'.

Sometimes errors occur because it is not immediately apparent whether the subject is singular or plural. The words listed below outside the brackets are all plural, although they may not look or sound it. Their singular forms are given inside the brackets.

criteria	(criterion)	strata	(stratum)
bacteria	(bacterium)	media	(medium)
phenomena	(phenomenon)	formulae	(formula)
radii	(radius)	*Note.* 'Formulas' is an alternative plural form.	

Notes on 'media', 'data' and 'index'

'Media' is the plural of 'medium', except when 'medium' is used in a spiritualist sense, such as 'seance mediums'.

'Data' is a plural word. The singular 'datum' is found in phrases such as 'datum point', the single point to which other data are compared or related. There is no absolute singular form, but 'one of the data' would be acceptable. Do not use 'data' simply as a more technical-sounding word for 'information'.

There are two plural forms for the singular 'index':

Indexes are found at the back of books etc., for example, indexes of names, subjects, etc.

Indices is the plural used in mathematics, economics and generally in technical subjects. Indices in mathematics are the little numbers representing 'powers'. There are indices of retail prices, the cost of living, wages and share prices.

Exercise 50

Correct these sentences where necessary.

(a) The bar graph is used to represent data that is either nominally or ordinally scaled.

(b) It is easy to work out the circumference of a circle once the length of a radii is known.

(c) If neither of these experimental methods are successful you must try a third one.

(d) The committee was divided in their opinions.

(e) In your assignments you may write 'none is' or 'none are'; either are acceptable.

(f) Adding the indexes is a method of multiplication in mathematics.

(g) Each of the units of measurement were originally natural units based on the lengths of certain parts of the human hand or foot.

(h) The action of bacterium break down the carbon compounds of plant systems to carbon dioxide and water.

(i) In a White Paper of 1970 a network of motorways for England of 4200 miles were proposed.

(j) What is your criteria for making such a judgement?

(k) The strata of relatively impermeable rocks that lie either above or below confined aquifers are called aquicludes.

(l) Either distribution through microwave radio links using tall towers or transmission from a satellite far above the surface of the earth are possible ways of disseminating television.

Confusing word pairs

Some pairs of words cause difficulty because they are spelt similarly and may sound similar or identical. Check the meanings of these words in your dictionary and attempt to complete the following exercise.

principal	principle
practice	practise
stationary	stationery
diffuse	defuse
compliment	complement
discrete	discreet
precede	proceed

Exercise 51

Choose the correct word from the pair given to complete the following sentences.

(a) In order to fit in her piano practice/practise, she had to miss the children's television programmes.

(b) Petroleum is the principle/principal raw material for plastic.

(c) With a practiced/practised flick of his wrist he threw the screwed up paper into his waste-paper basket.

(d) Since Liz's accident the team has been one player short of its compliment/complement.

(e) Libraries should have diffuse/defuse lighting otherwise the glare makes reading difficult.

(f) I knew I could confide in him because he is always discrete/discreet.

(g) The article always precedes/proceeds the noun to which it refers.

(h) The basic principal/principle of successful animal husbandry is quite simple: warmth and regular feeding.

(i) I would like to compliment/complement you on the skills you showed in dealing with the problem.

(j) Since London has become a target for terrorists, special units of police have been trained to diffuse/defuse bombs.

(k) Monogrammed stationery/stationary is an expensive luxury.

(l) It is always your fault if you collide with a stationery/stationary vehicle.

(m) Under the instructor's watchful eye she proceeded/preceded to demonstrate Hooke's law.

(n) A variable that can take only certain values is called a discrete/discreet variable.

Day six

Sentence structure: positioning words

We have been considering the essential parts of a sentence, the subject and verb. When other parts of speech are added the arrangement of the words becomes very important. In the two sentences:

> Water can be produced from steam. Steam can be produced from water.

the words are the same, but when they are reversed the meaning, the process taking place, is reversed too.

Often, however, the effect on meaning of the positioning of words is not as obvious as it is in the examples above. Placing words in their correct position requires more thought as the sentences become more complex.

A helpful hint for constructing complex sentences is to try, where possible, to place words associated together as near as possible to each other.

For example, the word 'only' when used as an adverb (i.e. modifying, or telling more about, the meaning of the verb) should be placed before its associated verb. What then do you think that this sentence means?

> I've only borrowed the books.

The writer may be intending to say either:

> It's just the books I've borrowed.

or   I've merely borrowed the books. (I've not stolen them, thrown them away, etc.)

Since 'only' comes before its verb, the sentence is to be understood as 'I've merely borrowed the books' and the other meaning is better expressed as 'I have borrowed only the books'.

Exercise 52

There are six possible positions for 'only' in the sentence given below. What are they and how is the meaning affected?

> I spoke to my tutor yesterday.

Relations within a sentence

In a sentence always keep items that are closely related in meaning close enough together to avoid doubt or ambiguity. Here is an example of a doubtfully arranged sentence:

> The boxer aimed a blow at his opponent's jaw, which slipped off and hit him on the shoulder.

Try writing this unambiguously.

It could be written:

> The blow, which the boxer had aimed at his opponents jaw, slipped off and hit his opponent's shoulder.

It is especially important to place pronouns as near as possible to the nouns they represent, otherwise the meaning can become confused.

Exercise 53

Rewrite these sentences to avoid confusion.

(a) The shark-spotting helicopter apparently failed to see the shark although it was circling over the bathers.

(b) As the guard went about his duties, he watched him closely, noting the time he came to feed him.

(c) I told my mother that she should help her.

(d) If the baby doesn't thrive on raw milk, boil it.

(e) There are some sticking plasters in my desk, which I keep for emergencies.

Day seven

Confusing words

Some words are confused with others because of similarities in their meaning or in the way they are used.

These are three pairs of words often confused:

less	fewer
comprise	constitute
lay	lie

Less refers to amount, quantity or extent and takes a singular noun. For example,

> The profit this year was less than last.

Fewer refers to number and is used with plural nouns. For example,

> There are fewer school leavers without jobs this year.

Comprise is equivalent to 'consist of'. For example,

> The accommodation offered comprised bedsitting room, kitchen and shared bathroom.

Note that 'comprise(d) of' is wrong.

Comprise can also mean 'compose' or 'make up'.

Constitute is equivalent to 'compose'. For example,

> Twelve people constituted the study group.

Lay means to put, to place and even to knock down, and its correct forms are *lay*, *laid*, *laid* (i.e. I might say 'I lay', 'I laid' or 'I have laid'). For example,

> Please lay down your pens.
> He laid the parcel on the table.

Notice that one always lays *something*.

Lie means to assume a recumbent position or to wait, and its correct forms are *lie*, *lay*, *lain*. For example,

> He felt faint and was obliged to lie down.
> They have lain in wait for the burglar now for three nights.

Exercise 54

Choose the correct word of those offered.

(a) There were less/fewer than twenty people present.

(b) The committee comprised/constituted the president of the club as chairman, the secretary, the treasurer and three elected members.

(c) 'I have run ten miles,' he said and laid/lay/lied down exhausted.

Who or whom?

Misuse of *who* and *whom* can cause a lot of confusion. The following three rules are presented as guidelines.

> *Rule 1*
> Use *who* when it is the subject (the doer) of a verb. For example,
>   I wish I knew who wrote it.

> *Rule 2*
> Use *whom* when it is the object (the person directly affected by the verb). For example,
>   Whom should I see when I arrived?

> *Rule 3*
> Use *whom* if it is governed by a preposition (to, from, by, etc.). For example,
>   'And therefore never send to know for whom the bell tolls'.

Exercise 55

Indicate by a tick or a cross whether you think each of these sentences is right or wrong.

(a) It is he to whom I had given my watch.

(b) Who have you got that from?

(c) This sentence is written by someone whom it appears is illiterate.

(d) The tenant whom we thought to be trustworthy has burnt the house down.

(e) Whom do you suppose is coming to tea?

Day eight

Nouns used as adjectives

It is quite common in modern English to use one noun to modify another, in other words, to use a noun as an adjective. Here are some examples:

> aluminium alloy
> wire bristles
> motor vehicles
> gas cylinder

However, it is also becoming commonplace to write strings of nouns together in the style of a newspaper headline rather than to use constructions containing prepositions. Consider this phrase:

> a national energy crisis conference

This could be written more clearly as:

> a conference on the crisis in national energy (supplies)

or perhaps the phrase means:

> a national conference on the crisis in energy (supplies)

This example demonstrates one of the shortcomings of this style of writing. Conciseness is gained at the expense of a clear indication of the exact relations between the words in the phrases. Here is another example:

> the world food production situation

which might mean:

> the amount and kinds of food produced throughout the world

although what, if anything, 'situation' means in this phrase is a completely open question.

Exercise 56

Rewrite these phrases to make their possible meaning clearer:

(a) specific diesel fuel system design variations

(b) overall information exchange complex

(c) domestic accommodation improvement programme

Day nine

Remember the guidance given earlier. When putting a sentence together you should try to place words most closely connected in the meaning of the sentence as near each other as possible.

Sometimes words that are intended to modify other words in a sentence are left unattached (without the support of the word they are supposed to modify).

Unattached participles

The present participle of a verb you will recognize as a form ending in *-ing* (like *ending*). The present participle always needs to be attached to some word that it modifies, as 'ending' was attached to 'form'. Consider this sentence:

> Looking out of the window, I saw an old friend walking down the street.

Here it is quite clear who is doing the looking ('I') and who is walking ('an old friend'). Now look at this example:

> Crossing the line, a train bumped into him.

In this sentence the writer wanted to say that it was the man who was crossing the line, but the grammar of the sentence suggests it was the train that was crossing the line. 'Crossing' is unattached, that is, it is without a word to which it can refer. The sentence could be altered to read:

> As he was crossing the line, a train bumped into him.

Similar problems can also occur with the past participle of a verb. A past participle of a verb is not quite so easy to recognize as a present participle. Although many verbs form their past participle with an *-ed*

80

ending (sometimes modified to -*t*), others have past participles ending in -*en* (e.g. broken), while for lots of common short verbs the past participle is either the same as the simple verb (e.g. run, hit) or is formed by changing the vowel in the middle (e.g. hung, got). Here is an example:

> Formal application is now being made for the necessary wayleave consent, and as soon as received the work will proceed.

The sentence construction is misleading. It suggests that the work, not the formal application, is to be received.

Exercise 57

Unattached participles are not always as obvious as they are in the examples above. Can you spot and correct what is wrong with these?

(a) We thank you for your order and, being always anxious to carry out our customers' wishes immediately, would you kindly state the address to which you wish the goods to be delivered.

(b) Whilst requesting you to furnish the return now outstanding you are advised that in future no further credit will be extended.

(c) Administered at first by the National Gallery, it was not until 1917 that the appointment of a separate board and director enabled a fully independent policy to be pursued.

(d) Arising out of a confrontation between the Government and the Opposition over devolution, Mrs Thatcher may seek an early vote of no confidence in the Government.

Please note: Some -*ing* words are now treated as acceptable on their own, that is unattached. This is usually because the unexpressed subject is indefinite, for example, 'one', 'people'. A few examples of these words are: regarding, considering, owing to, concerning, failing. The following then would be considered correct:

> Roughly speaking, present participles and gerunds are recognized by their -*ing* endings.

> Considering the attack that had been made on him, his speech was moderate in tone.

Day ten

Double negatives

In general double negatives are to be avoided. When spoken, a double negative is sometimes used to intensify a denial, although the rules of English grammar require the two halves of a double negative to cancel each other. Thus, 'I didn't see nothing' strictly means 'I did see something', although the speaker may have intended quite the opposite. If a negative meaning is required the sentence should contain only one negative and therefore should be either 'I saw nothing' or 'I didn't see anything'.

Double negatives can result from the use of 'scarcely' or 'hardly'. Both these words are indirectly negative and should be matched with a positive verb. For example,

> There *was* hardly any heating in the office.
> ('Was' is the positive verb.)

Not   There *wasn't* hardly any heating in the office.

It is possible to use double negatives correctly. Here's an example of one

82

type of double negative:

> It is only those who do nothing who make no mistakes.

This means the same as

> Everyone who does something makes mistakes sometimes.

Another kind of double negative makes use of an *un-* formation. Here are a couple of examples:

> The design of the building was not unattractive.
>
> I felt not unhappy about my answer.

In these examples the double negative does not mean the same as the direct positive, 'attractive' or 'happy', but instead a qualified or diminished positive. You should use this kind of double negative very sparingly. Used occasionally it can convey a precise shade of meaning, but repeated use creates a feeling of fussiness or simply of wordiness.

Exercise 58

Rewrite these sentences in the positive sense, but in such a way that they retain the literal meaning of the original sentences.

(a) He wasn't scarcely able to read the unit.

(b) 'I didn't say nothing,' she protested.

(c) It's not an unworkable solution.

(d) I couldn't not go.

(e) There is no one in this room who has not sometimes lied.

Split infinitives

The part of the verb called the infinitive is formed in English with *to* plus the verb-word itself (for example 'to study').

To split or not to split?

It is generally considered ill-advised to knowingly put a word or words between the *to* of the infinitive and the verb-word itself, as in this sentence: 'to knowingly put'. But sometimes, by avoiding splitting the infinitive, you end up making the sense of the sentence obscure or its expression clumsy.

Whether or not to split an infinitive really depends on the sentence in which it is found. Think about what this sentence means:

He began slowly to introduce new examples.

Is it his beginning that is slow or the introduction of new examples? If the first meaning is wanted, the sentence should be:

He slowly began to introduce new examples.

But if that is not what is meant, it would clarify the meaning to split the infinitive:

He began to slowly introduce new examples.

This is now clear, but so is:

He began to introduce new examples slowly.

Now consider another example:

They decided often to discuss political questions.

Again it might be preferable to split the infinitive, but this can be avoided and the meaning made clearer by writing:

They decided to discuss political questions often.

A split infinitive is hardly ever the only natural or even the most natural way to write what you mean.

Think: Can you move the word that splits the infinitive without changing the meaning? If so, do so.

Please note:

'To fully understand' is a split infinitive.
'To fully have understood' is a split infinitive.
'To have fully understood' is not a split infinitive.

So, if you are in doubt, try putting words like 'fully' after all parts of the verb you are using.

Exercise 59

Correct these sentences as necessary.

(a) It is the intention of the Minister of Transport to substantially increase all present rates by means of a general percentage.

(b) We intend to further support attempts at obtaining a truce.

(c) He seems to still be allowed to speak at unionist demonstrations.

(d) The greatest difficulty about assessing the economic achievements of the Soviet Union is that its spokesmen try to absurdly exaggerate them.

(e) Many of the workers are said to strongly favour a strike.

(f) It will be possible to considerably improve the wages of the workers.

Style

Day one

Repetition

Repetition usually occurs simply because concentration has lapsed. A word or phrase is repeated in the same sentence, or in the sentence immediately after, in a way that does not clarify the meaning but gives the reader an uncomfortable feeling. For example:

> The lecturer *also* mentioned the importance of the bicycle to the developing emancipation of women. He *also* included some material from an unpublished thesis.

In this example it would be better to omit the first *also*. Here is another:

> It is *essential* that you should be familiar with *essential* theories in the field.

In this case it would be better to change one of the *essential*s. The sentence might be rewritten as:

> It is absolutely necessary that you should be familiar with essential theories in the field.

Look at this final example:

> The increase in demand for *liquid oxygen* in the 1950s prompted the building of larger vehicles to carry the *liquid oxygen*.

Here it is better to replace the repeated phrase with a pronoun:

> The increase in demand for liquid oxygen in the 1950s prompted the building of larger vehicles to carry it.

When you are thinking about replacing a noun, that is, a 'naming' word with a pronoun, always check that there can be no doubt about which noun the pronoun stands for. (See 'Grammar', Day six.)

Exercise 60

Rewrite the following sentences so that repetition is avoided:

(a) Because I was late with my assignment because I found the calculations difficult, I didn't know whether my tutor would mark it.

(b) The Prime Minister went on to say that she hoped that everyone would cooperate with the new pay agreement. Her backbenchers went on to give the scheme unqualified support.

(c) If there is anything further I can do in the next few weeks to further the project, I will do it.

Latin phrases

There is nothing greatly superior about Latin phrases but their use is well established and you will come across them again and again in your reading. It's as well, therefore, to know the meanings of the most-used Latin phrases so that you understand them when you encounter them and use them correctly in your own writing if you wish.

Some of the best-known Latin phrases are used in abbreviated form. Below are three of the most common ones, together with the full Latin in brackets and the English meaning.

i.e. (*id est*)	that is
etc. (*et cetera*)	and other things
e.g. (*exempli gratia*)	for example

Here are examples of the use of each, with the English equivalent shown in brackets:

When working with any metal you must be aware of its various properties: malleability, conductivity, hardness, etc. (and other things).

Metal for forging must be malleable and ductile, i.e. (that is) able to be shaped without cracking when heated.

Metals used in forging are usually ferrous, e.g. (for example) wrought iron.

Small but important differences

It's important to understand that *i.e.* (that is) and *e.g.* (for example) are not interchangeable. The proper use of *e.g.* is to introduce *an example or examples*, as in this sentence:

> We need to be given more details of the accident, e.g. whether the operator was wearing the correct protective clothing.

On the other hand, *i.e.* introduces *another way of saying* what has already been said, driving home or clarifying the point that has been made:

> Do not use the components from this sealed box until absolutely necessary, i.e. when all other components have been used.

Exercise 61

Write the correct Latin abbreviations in the gaps in these sentences.

(a) Although different units of length – kilometre, centimetre, millimetre, _____ – are in common use, to avoid the possibilities of error all lengths should be given in metres.

(b) Computers have been used extensively in business to deal with routine and repetitive tasks, _____ lower-level clerical work.

(c) It is very often possible to draw opposite conclusions from the same facts because they have to be interpreted, _____ given meaning by the people observing them.

(d) The strike caused many inconveniences, _____ the refuse was not collected.

(e) If we are to take action we need proof of his having been party to the contract, _____ we need documentary or other conclusive evidence.

Day two

Redundancy

Redundancy is more difficult to detect than repetition because it is dependent on the meanings of the words, not just on the repeating of a word. Redundancy is a superfluity or excess; in writing, it is the use of more words than necessary to express the required meaning.

Take this example:

I shall continue to remain here.

Continue is implied in *remain*, so this sentence would be better as:

I shall remain here.

Here is another example:

There are desirable benefits to be gained from increasing research into alternative energy sources.

Benefits *are* desirable things, so 'desirable' is redundant.

Now consider these two sentences:

There is something about nuclear power stations that provokes anxiety.

There were a number of us who disagreed with your argument.

This way of beginning a sentence with a phrase like 'there is', 'there were' often adds nothing to the meaning and can be omitted, with a slight change to the rest of the sentence:

Something about nuclear power stations provokes anxiety.

A number of us disagreed with your argument.

Exercise 62

Pick out any words or phrases that are redundant in these sentences and rewrite where necessary.

(a) An attempt will be made today to try to achieve a settlement.

(b) There is a possibility that the mortar will crack.

(c) British people have never before in the past suffered so much from the effects of overeating.

(d) The building was constructed from modules, square in shape and all of the same dimensions.

(e) The subject of the discussion is about the role of government in scientific endeavour.

(f) The electrician explained the reason for the short in the circuit was because the water had dropped onto the wires.

Day three

Jargon

Jargon is usually ugly-sounding and difficult to understand, in fact the opposite of plain English. It involves the careless misuse or overuse of technical or semi-technical terms.

We read a lot of jargon every day in newspapers and hear it often in official pronouncements and public speaking. Here is an example given by Sir Ernest Gowers in *The Complete Plain Words* (p. 114):

> 'Manpower ceilings are a very blunt macro-instrument and will be either ineffective or unduly restrictive if not based on the results of management reviews and other 'micro' activities ... ceilings are biting, but this is what they were meant to do.'

It is not possible to interpret exactly what the writer means but the sentence could probably read:

> 'An overall restriction on manpower should only be applied when all details of the situation have been fully considered. Restrictions will bring difficulties but this is what they were meant to do.'

It may go unnoticed that words and phrases of jargon are cluttering sentences and obscuring the meaning. Try to use technical words only when they express precisely what you want to say. Don't use them just because they come most readily to mind; that is what turns them into jargon.

You may find Exercise 63 difficult, but this should help to convince you of why jargon is to be avoided. Don't worry if you are not able to rewrite the sentences in plain English; refer to the answers where necessary. You will at least have learnt how jargon can obscure meaning.

Exercise 63

Rewrite these sentences clearly, without the jargon.

(a) The most efficient form of price control is a competitive situation where competitive pressures ensure the maximum productivity of factor inputs.

(b) A grass-roots confrontation took place between the different unions representing the workers in the tool shop.

(c) A meaningful discussion was held within the frame of reference suggested by the negotiator for the dockers.

(d) The depot is designed for integrated road and rail freight as a direct result of a developmental feasibility study.

(e) A one-off meeting was arranged between the two leaders.

(f) They discussed a thought-provoking article which looked at the on-going importance of the green pound to British agriculture.

(g) Annual repayments will be geared to the individual's cash flow.

(h) A viable long-term structure needs to be taken into account when investment decisions are made.

(i) The essential requirement for British agriculture is to be in a state of preparedness to respond to demand both in the UK and overseas and to make a maximum contribution to national wealth creation.

(j) My profit-oriented views were not acceptable to the Board.

Day four

Technical language

Some technical language is often necessary to express precisely what a 'specialist' writer has to convey to his reader. There's nothing wrong with using technical terms freely in their correct context. Sentence structure should be kept as simple as the subject matter will allow. Here's an example of how an obscure piece of technical writing can be written more simply and clearly. This is the original:

> Undue attachment to the thesis that inflation is the result solely of institutional factors might cause the contribution made to inflation by excess demand to be neglected and the existence of excess demand to be prolonged.

Here is a simpler, clearer version:

> Inflation is caused not only by institutional factors but also by excess demand, and unless we recognize this and act on it excess demand is likely to continue.

Think: Are you using technical language merely to impress your reader? The point made by Gowers in *The Complete Plain Words* is worth remembering: 'No sensible reader supposes that what is easy to understand must have been easy to think of.'

Exercise 64

Rewrite these sentences as simply as possible while retaining the original meaning. (My answers will naturally differ from yours.)

(a) By selecting extrapolations of current or emerging tendencies that grow continuously out of today's world, and reflect the multifold trend and our current expectations, we create a 'surprise-free' projection – one that seems less surprising than any other specific possibility.

(b) Although certain broad zonational patterns are discernible in the geographical distribution of animals as well as in those of soils and vegetation, the mobility of animals and, in the case of some, seasonal altitudinal migrations mean that the zonation becomes indistinct.

Day five

Cliché

It is when you are searching for a word or phrase to express an idea neatly and succinctly that you will be most tempted to use a cliché. Clichés are phrases, or sometimes single words, that have become worn out through overuse. The original user of the particular phrase may have said something illuminating and apt. Subsequent users 'borrow' the phrase on every possible occasion, and it becomes meaningless. Clichés are frequently found in everyday conversation and because of their familiarity you may use them in your writing without realizing that you are doing so.

For example, the sentence:

> The motion was *well and truly* defeated when put to the vote.

could have been written:

> The motion was easily defeated when put to the vote.

Exercise 65

These sentences contain some typical clichés. Either write a better phrase to replace the cliché, or rewrite the sentence completely, eliminating the cliché but retaining the original sense.

(a) The Chancellor announced that as a result of the improved economic situation a wave of optimism was sweeping the country.

(b) The shop steward made a public statement to the effect that the management's refusal to come to the bargaining table was the thin edge of the wedge.

(c) It would be a sad day for Britain if irresponsible wage claims paved the way to ever-rising inflation.

(d) Time and again you will encounter examples of narrow specialism, where problems have been solved in a limited context without a look at the wider consequences of the solutions or the ways and means used to achieve them.

(e) In the framework of the Race Relations Act, such tests could be challenged for the first time as a form of indirect discrimination.

Day six

Metaphor

Metaphor is a way of making an idea or description vivid. It does this by a comparison or transfer of meaning from one thing to another. To be effective a metaphor must be apt.

Try to pick out all the metaphors in this sentence:

> The Government machine has become increasingly intricate, and Number Ten thus becomes the single ganglion of the nervous system, the apex of the pyramid, the only office which really knows everything that is going on.

It is obvious that the writer is trying to make a forceful point about how complex the Government workings have become. He tries to do this by using several metaphors, but these are quite unrelated to each other and evoke a series of confusing and rather ludicrous images in the reader.

Extensive use of such metaphors often produces a ridiculous effect, for example,

> The Rt Hon. Gentleman is leading the people over the precipice with his head in the sand.

Exercise 66

Here are some examples of mixed metaphors. For each example write a couple of sentences pointing out the confusions.

(a) The wind of change is threatening to explode the stability of the currency system.

(b) Flexibility is one of the corner-stones of our new programme.

(c) Their political opponents had proferred the olive branch, but nothing concrete had come out of it.

(d) What I have to do is to see that our organization is built upon a solid foundation, never allowing the possibility of the Society's life-blood being sapped.

Day seven

Here are some more notes on technical language and familiar words and phrases.

Overused and abused terms

Beware of technical terms that are transferred incorrectly into everyday speech and writing. Also, look out for the many words in English that have a precise meaning, but which are used carelessly without regard to their real meaning.

In this sentence the word 'crucial' is used correctly:

> The meeting of the heads of departments to consider the proposed degree courses will be the crucial one.

But here it is not:

> A speedy end to widespread unemployment is crucial for our economy.

'Crucial' means decisive or critical. It would have been better to write:

> A speedy end to widespread unemployment is most important for our economy.

If you are unsure about a word, check its meaning in your dictionary and then look critically at the use to which it is put. You may find you need your dictionary for the next exercise.

Exercise 67

Each pair of sentences provides a correct and an incorrect use of a word. For each pair, tick the sentence which uses the word correctly and say what is wrong about its use in the incorrect sentence.

(a) (i) For an hour or two yesterday I had a really chronic headache.

  (ii) Through all those years he was always good-tempered and serene, even though he was a chronic invalid.

(b) (i) I hate filling in forms; I must be allergic to them because I always get something wrong in them.

(ii) After years of suffering from a hayfever-like irritation he was found to be allergic to the fur of his own pet cat.

(c) (i) A generous donation from the company facilitated the whole research project.

(ii) The research student was facilitated by an extremely helpful archivist.

(d) (i) After the terrorist attack, they anticipated that new and stricter security regulations would be imposed.

(ii) He saw that they had anticipated success by opening the magnum of champagne before the results of the competition were known.

Familiar and meaningless?

It is necessary to think carefully about using very familiar words or phrases. The next exercise is to give you more practice in 'noticing' familiar words used incorrectly; some have no meaning at all in the sentence in which they are found.

Think: In your writing, do such words express what you want to say or have they lost impact and become vague?

Exercise 68

Correct these sentences where you think necessary.

(a) A man of his proportions would break such a flimsy chair.

(b) I am in receipt of your letter of 4th inst. and will be replying as soon as I have any information for you.

(c) The proceedings of the tribunal were held *in camera*.

(d) There is every indication that the new corporation will be a tower of strength and forge ahead.

(e) These investigations will be an essential input to the process of assessing market trends.

(f) This document is forwarded herewith for the favour of your utilization.

(g) The bankruptcy of Rolls-Royce produced a national trauma without real precedent.

A brief note on slang

Most slang results from play with words. Although slang is prevalent in everyday speech, it is rarely precise enough to be appropriate in essays and assignments. In writing, slang is found in journalism, particularly sporting journalism. Here it has become more acceptable, but you are not likely to find slang acceptable in your essays.

Bibliographies and references

Exercise 69

Write down very briefly what you think a bibliography is. To check what you have written, look up the word 'bibliography' in your dictionary. Check also in the answers section of *Plain English*. If necessary, correct or fill out your description.

When you are writing an essay, you may want to direct your reader's (primarily, your tutor's) attention to a particular figure, table, equation or passage of text in some book or article. Similarly, an author of your course material may wish to refer you to some particular item within a book or article (or, at least, give you the opportunity of looking it up if you choose to). The entries in a bibliography relate to complete works, that is, to whole books or articles. In order to find a particular figure or passage of text within the complete work, more details will be needed. The total information required to pinpoint a particular item – the information for the complete work given in the bibliography, and the detailed information such as page and figure numbers – is what I mean by the *reference* for that item.

1   How to describe a book for a bibliography

The prime reason for including a book in a bibliography is to enable an interested person to locate the book. Normally one would go to a library to do this, and this is the principal way in which bibliographies are designed to be used. The information in an entry in a bibliography should also be sufficient to allow one to buy or to order the book from a bookshop.

A basic description of a book contains the following four pieces of information:

  (i) author's (or editor's) name,
 (ii) title (underlined),
(iii) publisher,
(iv) year of publication.

The detailed arrangement of these four bits of information may vary a little, but the basic arrangement is like this:

> D. Barber (ed.), *Farming and Wildlife*, Royal Society for the Protection of Birds, 1970.
>
> P. Gaskell, *A New Introduction to Bibliography*, Clarendon Press, 1972.
>
> W. C. Patterson, *Nuclear Power*, Penguin, 1976.

Notice that the first word and all the main words in the book's title begin with a capital letter. Also notice that titles of books are *printed in italics*. In writing they should be underlined because underlining something in writing means exactly the same as printing it in italics. Indeed, the way to indicate to a printer that you want something printed in italics is just to underline it in the typescript.

Exercise 70

Write descriptions of the following three books as for a bibliography:

(a) In 1968 David & Charles published an illustrated history of *The Kennet & Avon Canal* written by Kenneth R. Clew.

(b) There is a book called *Population Dynamics* by Maurice E. Solomon, which Edward Arnold published in 1969.

(c) M.P. Crosland has edited a comprehensive survey of theories of matter from ancient Greece to the present day; it was published by Penguin in 1971 with the title *The Science of Matter*.

If you have a book that you want to describe for a bibliography, where do you find the essential bits of information? The title, the name of the author or editor, and the publisher's name appear on the title page. The year of publication may also appear on the title page; otherwise you will find it on the back of the title page. Many books have a page before the title page called the 'half-title'; the information contained on the half-title varies and the only constant feature is probably the book's title itself.

Exercise 71

Now take three of your own books and write their descriptions as for a bibliography.

(i)

(ii)

(iii)

If you had any difficulty fitting any of your descriptions to the basic form I have outlined, you might like to turn straight away to section 4 'Additional information', where complications like editions and translations are dealt with.

2   Useful abbreviations for bibliographies and references

Before going on to the description of papers and articles for a bibliography you will need to know a few of the common abbreviations frequently used in bibliographies and references. I shall simply list them here, and you can practise using them in later exercises.

ch(s).	chapter(s)
ed(s).	editor(s); edited by
edn	edition
eq.	equation
et al.	(Latin, = *et alii*) and others – used when there are more than two authors or editors

fig(s).	figure(s)
fn.	footnote
l., ll.	line, lines
no(s).	number(s)
p., pp.	page, pages
rev.	revised (by)
tr.	translator; translated (by)
vol(s).	volume(s)

3 How to describe papers and articles for a bibliography

(a) Papers or articles published in a book

The basic description has the following information:

 (i) author's name,
 (ii) title of paper or article (within quotation marks),
 (iii) details of the book as described in section 1: editor's name, title of book (underlined), publisher, year of publication,
 (iv) page numbers of first and last pages of paper or article.

Again, the details may vary slightly, but here are two examples of the basic arrangement:

> G.M. Clemence, 'Time measurement for scientific use', in J.T. Fraser (ed.), *The Voices of Time*, Allen Lane The Penguin Press, 1968, pp. 401–14.

> R.W. Page, 'Population forecasting', in H.S.D. Cole *et al.* (eds.), *Thinking about the Future*, Chatto & Windus/Sussex University Press, 1973, pp. 159–74.

(b) Papers or articles published in journals or periodicals

Journals and periodicals are usually published at regular intervals over a period of many years. They are often bound up in volumes for keeping in libraries. Full details are therefore needed if an article is to be found easily. The basic description requires the following information:

 (i) author's name,
 (ii) title of paper or article (within quotation marks),
 (iii) title of journal or periodical (underlined and with capital first letters of main words),
 (iv) volume number,

(v) issue number (not all journals have these),
(vi) date of issue (see below),
(vii) page numbers of first and last pages of paper or article.

The details of date depend on the frequency with which the journal is published. The year of publication is essential. For a quarterly or monthly journal, the season or month of issue is useful, but not essential if the issue number is given; for a weekly publication (e.g. *New Scientist* or *Nature*), the full date of issue is of more use than the issue number.

Here are some examples:

> A.C. Rose-Innes, 'The new superconductors', *Contemporary Physics*, vol. 7, no. 2, 1965, pp. 135–51.

> J. Stansell, 'North Sea gas – an ever changing pipedream', *New Scientist*, vol. 79, no. 1113, 27 July 1978, pp. 264–5.

> J.P.R. Williams and B. McGibbon, 'Cervical spine injuries in Rugby Union football', *British Medical Journal*, no. 6154, 23–30 December 1978, p. 1747.

There is a point to note about page numbers: these should be given with the minimum number of figures consistent with the pronunciation. You will see in the previous examples that I have written, '401–14', '159–74', '135–51', '264–5', in each case not repeating the figures that remain the same. On the other hand, one would write, '13–17' or '215–19', because of the way you would read these aloud. For similar reasons, one should write, '100–104' or '50–51'.

Exercise 72

Write descriptions for a bibliography of the following articles:

(a) The 1978 Richard Dimbleby Lecture was delivered by Lord Rothschild; he called it 'Risk'. The text was published in the *Listener* on 30 November 1978 from p. 715 to p. 718; that issue was designated volume 100, no. 2588.

(b) D. Nicholls wrote a review article called 'Theories of acids and bases', which was published in the journal *Chemistry Student* in 1967. It runs from p. 33 to p. 38 of issue no. 2 of volume 1 of the journal. The same article was subsequently reprinted on pp. 191–204 of a book called

Modern Chemistry edited by J.G. Stark and published by Penguin in 1970. (Write two separate descriptions.)

---

4   Additional information

It is often the case that a book which is in print for a number of years is revised from time to time and the publisher brings out a new edition. When listing such a book in a bibliography, it is important to make sure that your reader can find the same edition that you have referred to. You will often find the edition number printed on the cover of a book, but the best place to look is on the back of the title page, where the book's 'publishing history' is given. Ignore all the reprintings that are not given new edition numbers, and find the latest edition number and the corresponding date: that is the edition you are handling. Here are just two examples:

> J.E. Gordon, *The New Science of Strong Materials* (2nd edn), Penguin, 1976.

> B. Mason, *Principles of Geochemistry* (3rd edn), Wiley, 1966.

A book with a single author may be translated or edited by someone else. The latter case is not likely to be encountered among technical works, unless you start delving into the 'collected works' of some nineteenth-century founding father, but you may occasionally find yourself reading a translation. Here is just one example:

> M. Born, *The Restless Universe* (2nd edn), tr. W.M. Deans, Dover, 1951.

In section 3(a) I gave an example of a book with two publishers, *Thinking about the Future*, published by Chatto & Windus on behalf of Sussex University Press. You may notice that 'course readers' for some Open University courses are published by a commercial publisher on behalf of the Open University Press. Here is another example of a joint publication:

> J.L. Lewis (ed.), *Teaching School Physics*, Penguin/UNESCO, 1972.

Exercise 73

Convert the following information into a bibliography, arranging the entries in alphabetical order of first author's (editor's) names.

There is an article on 'Earthquake prediction and modification' by Robert L. Kovach in *Understanding the Earth*, which was edited by I.G. Gass, Peter J. Smith and R.C.L. Wilson. It runs from p. 327 to p. 332 in the second edition, which was published in 1972 for the Open University Press by Artemis Press.

A Short History of Technology by T.K. Derry and Trevor I. Williams was first issued as an Oxford University Press paperback in 1970.

Recently my wife bought me an early copy of the Pelican *Metals in the Service of Man* by William Alexander and Arthur Street from our local Oxfam shop; it is the third edition, published by Penguin in 1946.

In volume 10, issue no. 3 of *Contemporary Physics*, published in 1969, there is an article called 'Electrolysis and simple cells' by R. Parsons on pp. 205–20.

The third level course *Control of Technology* has a course reader entitled *The Politics of Technology* edited by Godfrey Boyle, David Elliott and Robin Roy and published by Longman in association with the Open University Press in 1977.

When I was trying to study mathematics I used a book called *Principles of Dynamics* by B.M. Glauert, published by Routledge & Kegan Paul in 1960.

In 1966 a paper by M.F. Hoyaux entitled 'Plasma physics and its applications' appeared in volume 7, issue no. 4, of the journal *Contemporary Physics*, beginning on p. 241 and ending on p. 260.

Answers to exercises

Punctuation

Exercise 1

Brunel's critics still refused to be convinced and now maintained that when the time came to remove the centering altogether the bridge would surely collapse. The engineer himself had no doubts whatever about his bridge but he ruled that the centres should not be removed finally until it had stood through another winter. The suspicion that this was due not so much to excessive caution as to an impish sense of humour is hard to resist. Certainly the fact that the bridge was standing entirely free for nine months while his jealous opponents supposed that the centering was still helping to support it was a joke that Brunel must have relished keenly. Its point was revealed and his critics confounded by a violent storm one autumn night in 1839 which blew all the useless centering down. (L.T.C. Rolt, *Isambard Kingdom Brunel*, Penguin, 1970, p. 172.)

Exercise 2

For each sentence answer (i) indicates the least number of full stops that is consistent with good modern practice; answer (ii) is an equally acceptable version with all the possible full stops added.

(a) (i) Mr and Mrs J.B. Jones, who live at 23 St James's Gardens, told PC Alderbank that they had been woken at 3 a.m. by the sound of glass breaking and had seen a man running out of the house opposite, no. 26.

(ii) Mr. and Mrs. J.B. Jones, who live at 23 St. James's Gardens, told P.C. Alderbank that they had been woken at 3 a.m. by the sound of glass breaking and had seen a man running out of the house opposite, no. 26.

(b) (i) Radio programmes for the OU are broadcast on VHF only; TV programmes are broadcast on either BBC2 or BBC1.

(ii) Radio programmes for the O.U. are broadcast on V.H.F. only; T.V. programmes are broadcast on either B.B.C.2 or B.B.C.1.

(c) (i) In March 1979 the Royal Society held a discussion meeting on nuclear magnetic resonance (n.m.r.) of intact biological systems organized by Prof. R.J.P. Williams, FRS, Prof. E.R. Andrew and Dr G.K. Radda.

(ii) In March 1979 the Royal Society held a discussion meeting on nuclear magnetic resonance (n.m.r.) of intact biological systems organized by Prof. R.J.P. Williams, F.R.S., Prof. E.R. Andrew and Dr. G.K. Radda.

Exercise 3

Within the wider community of British universities the Open University is the only institution that demands no entrance qualifications of its students. This means, however, that foundation courses have to play a crucial role in its teaching system. They form the bridge between students of enormously varied educational backgrounds and the higher-level courses that will enable them to become graduates.

In designing *Living with Technology* the Course Team paid almost as much attention to the course's role as a foundation course as to the fact that it is a course about *technology*. (T101 *Living with Technology, Introduction*, 2nd edn, p. 23.)

Exercise 4

The Castner cell underwent various slight modifications during the first quarter of the century, but in 1924 the American J.C. Downs patented a cell for the production of sodium from fused sodium chloride. This consisted of a steel tank lined with firebrick containing a massive cylindrical graphite anode projecting through the base, surrounded coaxially by a cathode of iron gauze. By adding calcium chloride to the sodium chloride, the melting-point of the electrolyte is reduced from 800 °C to 505 °C. The energy efficiency of the Downs cell process from salt to sodium is about three times greater than that of the composite process of first producing sodium hydroxide in a mercury cell, followed by further electrolysis in a Castner cell. However, both processes were in operation in 1950. The price of sodium in the U.S.A. dropped from $2.00 per pound in 1890 to $0.15 per pound in 1946. (T.I. Williams, ed., *A History of Technology*, vol. 6, Oxford University Press, 1978, pp. 519–21.)

Do not worry if you were not aware that Castner is a personal name. Also, the full stops in U.S.A. are quite optional; USA is equally correct.

Exercise 5

(a) Your home might be heated by solid fuel, oil, gas or electricity. (*Alternatively:* ... solid fuel, oil, gas, or electricity.)

(b) Resources are defined as energy, materials, labour and capital. (*Or:* ... labour, and capital.)

(c) He found he needed several metres of electric cable, three junction boxes, a packet of insulated staples, four light switches and an assortment of tools. (*Or:* ... four light switches, and an assortment of tools.)

Exercise 6

(a) Copper is a malleable, ductile metal.

(b) Many new electronic gadgets have appeared in recent years.

(c) The new crystals tended to be long, smooth, whip-like filaments.

Exercise 7

(a) The engine stalled, the brakes failed and the car started to roll backwards.

(b) Britain now has a system as advanced as any in the world, and other countries are adopting similar measures.

(c) I was finding it hard to keep up with the course and had missed one or two television programmes, but I made a point of going to all the tutorials and sending in my assignments on time.

(d) Seaside habitats are equally rich and provide great contrasts in species.

Exercise 8

(a) All matter is made up of atoms and all atoms are made up of an inner nucleus (plural: nuclei) surrounded by electrons. Almost the whole mass of the atom is concentrated in the nucleus, but the nucleus is much smaller than the whole atom. The bulk of the nucleus is made up of protons and neutrons. All the atoms of a particular chemical element contain the same number of protons, and this number is known as the atomic number of the element. The atomic number of hydrogen is 1, that of carbon is 6 and that of oxygen is 8. This means that all hydrogen atoms contain 1 proton, all carbon atoms contain 6 protons and all oxygen atoms contain 8 protons.

(b) The pressure, volume and temperature of a fixed quantity of gas are interrelated. Boyle's law states that at constant temperature the volume of a given mass of gas is inversely proportional to the pressure, and Charles's law states that at constant pressure the volume of a given mass of gas is directly proportional to the absolute temperature. For a mole of gas these two laws may be combined in the gas equation $pV = RT$. In this equation p is the pressure, V is the volume, R is the gas constant and T is the absolute temperature. Gases do not strictly obey the gas laws, but follow them more and more closely as the pressure of the gas is reduced.

Exercise 9

(a) Heavy chemicals are essentially those produced in bulk and used in large quantities; fine chemicals are made on a comparatively small scale, some indeed in quantities of only a pound or two. (T.I. Williams, *The Chemical Industry*, Penguin, 1953, p. 120.)

(b) However, technology does not make the only claim on manpower; planning, to be mentioned in a moment, also requires a comparatively high level of specialized talent. (J.K. Galbraith, *The New Industrial State*, 2nd edn, Deutsch, 1972, p. 15; Penguin edn, 1974, p. 34.)

(c) Fox Talbot's sensitive material, like Daguerre's, was silver iodide, formed not more than a day before use as a thin film on paper which was brushed successively with solutions of silver nitrate and potassium iodide; the sensitivity to light was increased by further treatment with gallic acid, the sensitizing properties of this having been discovered in 1837 by J.B. Reade, another British pioneer. (*A Short History of Technology*, p. 655.)

Exercise 10

Although this branch of the chemical industry is the one with which the general public most frequently comes into direct contact it is nevertheless one about which many misconceptions exist. Plastics are often spoken of as though there was little difference between the various kinds; in fact they differ enormously in their properties. Plastics are often thought of as new substances; in fact they have been in use for a century. Plastics are often regarded as cheap substitutes for other and better constructional materials such as wood, metal, and natural textiles; in fact many have found favour on their own merits and often are far from cheap. (*The Chemical Industry*, p. 173.)

You may, of course, omit the comma after 'metal' in the last sentence.

Exercise 11

(a) The steelworkers' representative, a foundryman from Humberside, argued for rapid modernization.

(b) It was his spelling, not his punctuation, that he needed to improve.

(c) He had, no doubt, a speech carefully prepared for the occasion.

(d) There are two alternatives for punctuating this sentence, depending on the way 'however' is being used:

(i) These incidents, however trivial in themselves, are liable to lead to more serious demonstrations.

(ii) These incidents, however, trivial in themselves, are liable to lead to more serious demonstrations.

Exercise 12

(a) The fire having been lit for some time, the room was quite warm.

(b) The fire, having been lit for some time, needed stoking.

(c) Obtaining planning permission for this factory will not be easy.
Or:
Obtaining planning permission, for this factory, will not be easy. (The addition of the commas emphasizes the difficulty in the case of this particular factory.)

(d) The results of his early experiments being positive, he was encouraged to embark on a more ambitious programme of research.

(e) The charge on the anode, being positive, attracts the negatively charged anions.

Exercise 13

Tyres, of course, have the function of spreading and cushioning the load beneath the wheels of a vehicle, and in this they are extremely successful. However, tyres are really only one example of a whole class of blown-up structures. Quite apart from any cushioning effects, blown-up structures provide a very effective way of evading the serious penalties in weight and cost which are incurred when we try to carry light loads over a long distance in bending or in compression. (J.E. Gordon, *Structures*, Penguin, 1978, pp. 314–15.)

Exercise 14

(a) Four types of malt whisky are made in Scotland: Campbeltown, Highland, Islay and Lowland. (*Or:* ... Islay, and Lowland.)

(b) Time is short: sixteen months is not a long time.

(c) Charles Darwin wrote: 'I am convinced that Natural Selection has been the main but not exclusive means of modification.'

Exercise 15

Chapman develops three basic scenarios for future patterns of fuel demands in Britain: 'business-as-usual', 'technical-fix', and 'low-growth' scenarios. These represent, respectively: the virtually unrestrained projection of present trends, the introduction of some technical changes to effect a more moderate growth in fuel demand, and more radical proposals to effect a very definite restriction in the growth of fuel demand and aimed eventually at stabilizing demand. For each case, Chapman explores how the various components of total fuel demand would change, and the policy options that would need to be exercised to supply the various demands. This exploration is succinctly conveyed, but rests on considerable analysis and Chapman's specialist knowledge of energy demands and the fuel industries. (The Open University, T361 *Control of Technology*, Unit 8, The Open University Press, 1978, p. 14.)

Exercise 16

(a) If you are not confident about your spelling, turn to the next section of this booklet, where you will find some useful spelling tests and exercises.

(b) When you have studied energy in more detail, as you will do later in this course, you will realize how often in your everyday life you use energy-conversion devices, of which the electric kettle is a familiar example.

Exercise 17

(a) Describing: 'who by now was only a few yards off'.
Defining: 'whom I had seen that morning at the inn'.

(b) Defining: 'where I was born'.

(c) Defining: 'when beer was twopence a pint'.

(d) Describing: 'where we are opening a new factory'.

Exercise 18

(a) People who live in country districts are particularly affected by the withdrawal of bus services.
Defining: 'who live in country districts'.

(b) I want you to know the basic rules which govern punctuation.
Defining: 'which govern punctuation'.

(c) In this book he gives a very balanced account of nuclear power, which I think you should read.
Describing: 'which I think you should read'.

(d) It was a letter from my mother, who was worried because I had not written lately.
Describing: 'who was worried because I had not written lately'. (I do not need to define my mother.)

(e) Usually my brother met me at the station, but on that memorable Friday it was my father who came to meet me.
Defining: 'who came to meet me'.

How can this be a defining clause? I do not have several fathers, of whom this is one. The key to the riddle lies in the word 'it'. In (d) you will see immediately that 'it' is 'a letter', but in (e) 'it' does not seem to be anything at all. What the sentence really means is something like: 'Usually my brother met me at the station, but on that memorable Friday the person who came to meet me was my father.' So the person that 'who came to meet me' defines is not actually in the sentence.

I put this exercise in to make the point that although I have tried to present you with simple rules to help you with your punctuation and have tried to choose examples and exercises to exemplify these rules, in fact the English language refuses to be bound by simple rules, and so the guidance I can offer you is bound to be limited.

Exercise 19

Although bats flourish and survive very well today, pterodactyls were superseded by birds, which have feathers, a great many years ago. It is possible, of course, that the extinction of pterodactyls had nothing to do with structural considerations, but it is also possible that there is something special about feathers which gives birds an edge over other flying creatures. When I worked at the Royal Aircraft Establishment I used to ask my superiors, from time to time, whether it would not perhaps be better if aeroplanes had feathers; but I seldom succeeded in extracting a rational or even a patient answer to this question. (*Structures*, p. 129.)

Exercise 20

(a) the amplifier's gain
(b) the amplifiers' gains
(c) chemistry's importance
(d) the gas's properties
(e) the gases' properties
(f) the men's occupations

Exercise 21

(a) Its roof was insulated.
(b) It's too early for the pubs to be open.
(c) I must have overloaded its circuits.
(d) Its main disadvantage is its weight.
(e) It's the latest model and its performance is second to none.
(f) It's not easy to understand relativity theory because its concepts are mathematical.

Exercise 22

Why have I called the package a 'unit'? Because it represents a week's worth of your time: one week of student study is the basic unit of the Open University's arithmetic. The remainder of this course is built around a set of 'blocks', each of which contains several units' worth of work. Studying each unit will involve not just reading text, but also watching television, listening to radio, working through audiovision and answering assignments. (T101 *Living with Technology, Introduction*, p. 5.)

Exercise 23

'Polychlorinated biphenyls (PCBs) should be regarded as if they were carcinogenic to humans', says a report by the International Agency for Research on Cancer (*IARC Monographs*, vol. 18). But the authoritative and cautious IARC says there is insufficient evidence to decide whether polybrominated biphenyls (PBBs), the close chemical cousins of PCBs, are also carcinogenic. (*New Scientist*, 11 January 1979, p. 78.)

Exercise 24

Figure 16 shows the pattern of energy flow in the United Kingdom. In 1975 gross consumption of *primary energy* in the United Kingdom was approximately 2425 TWh (1 TWh = 10^9 kWh). But, because of inefficiencies in energy conversion and distribution, some 30 per cent or so (725 TWh) is lost between producer and consumer. Even when this *delivered energy* finally arrives at the point of consumption, further losses of around 30 per cent (725 TWh) occur in the appliances and processes in which it is used. Central-heating boilers, for instance, have efficiencies of only 60 per cent or so, open coal fires are even worse, with a typical efficiency of only 20 per cent, and motor cars with internal combustion engines are still less efficient (less than 20 per cent). (T361 *Control of Technology*, Units 10–11, p. 68.)

Exercise 25

(a) The start of the second phase of the three-year programme was set back a month.

(b) This will be a set-back for your far-fetched schemes; perhaps it will bring you down to earth.

(c) This recently published report contains up-to-date information on low-level radiation leaks from advanced gas-cooled reactors.

Exercise 26

On the other hand, the *unit* costs (or 'run-on costs') of printing the magazine on a hand-operated duplicating machine will be relatively high, for various reasons:

(a) The machine, because it is hand operated, can produce relatively few copies per hour, so the labour cost of each copy is relatively high.

(b) The machine, for technical reasons, has to use fairly heavy paper, which makes the cost of each copy relatively high. Also the stencil, being made of waxed paper, will break up after, say, a thousand copies or so, and a new one will have to be typed.

(c) The machine prints only one page at a time, so that when all the sheets (thirty-two of them for a sixty-four-page magazine) are finally printed it takes a long time to collate them by hand and staple them into a magazine. (T361 *Control of Technology*, Units 10–11, p. 53.)

Exercise 27

(a) (i) No one has yet built a living organism (however simple) starting from scratch.

(ii) No one has yet built a living organism, however simple, starting from scratch.

Commas give the best effect here.

(b) (i) A combination of three types of study (two on humans and one on animals) indicates strongly that alcohol is harmful to unborn babies.

(ii) A combination of three types of study, two on humans and one on animals, indicates strongly that alcohol is harmful to unborn babies.

Perhaps the case for brackets is stronger than for (a), but I still prefer the commas.

Exercise 28

(a) The Chinese are thrifty people: the earth dug out was used to make bricks for the tunnel walls.

(b) Already it has sold six systems: three in Denmark, two in Spain and one in Italy.

In both these examples I prefer the colon.

Exercise 29

This is how I would punctuate the passage:

A purely inorganic compound with optical activity, the first for almost 50 years, has just been synthesized by Robert Gillard and Franz Winmer of University College, Cardiff. Most known optically active compounds – molecules with structures that cannot be superimposed upon their mirror image – contain carbon atoms. They are either organic compounds or chelates, i.e. complexes of transition metals where the carbon atoms help form the claw-like ligands.

The pair of dashes that I have retained mark off an explanation of the term 'optically active compounds' that is inserted in the middle of the sentence. If such an explanation occurred at the end of a sentence, it could be introduced by a colon, but this cannot be done in the middle of a sentence because there is no suitable punctuation mark to end such an explanation. This is where dashes are most useful.

You may think I cheated by inserting an 'i.e.' in place of the last dash. I do not think a colon will do here because the words after the dash (in the original) define only the word 'chelates'. Another solution is to put the definition in brackets.

You will see I also omitted the comma before 'or'; a comma is not required in a simple 'either ... or ...' phrase like this.

All the examples in the section on the dash were taken from *New Scientist*. I suspect that the staff writers and editors on *New Scientist* favour the dash because they feel it has an informal air about it that the colon and semicolon certainly do not have, and that informality is appropriate to their journalistic style.

Exercise 30

(a) It is found that meteors fall into two distinct classes: the stony and the iron–nickel types, with a few intermediate or stony–iron types. (E.F. Slade, *Interfaces of Physics*, Penguin, 1973, p. 130.)

(b) The Beer–Lambert law is an extension of a law proposed by Lambert in 1760, which stated that layers of equal thickness of a homogeneous material absorb equal proportions of light. (*Interfaces of Physics*, p. 28.)

(c) Einstein suggested that the path of a particle in four-dimensional space–time is a geodesic.

Spelling

Exercise 31

(a) beginning
(b) allotted
(c) benefited
(d) compelling

Exercise 32

(a) wrong   successful
(b) right
(c) wrong   occasionally
(d) wrong   committee
(e) wrong   exaggerate
(f) wrong   abbreviate
(g) wrong   parallel
(h) wrong   omission
(i) right
(j) right

Exercise 33

(a) achieved
(b) quotient
(c) deficient
(d) ceiling
(e) perceive

Exercise 34

(a) right
(b) wrong   accelerator
(c) right
(d) wrong   inventor
(e) wrong   distributor
(f) right

Exercise 35

(a) substances
(b) recurrence
(c) inferences
(d) resistance
(e) performance

Exercise 36

(a) homogeneous
(b) nutritious
(c) precarious
(d) meticulous
(e) numerous
(f) erroneous
(g) cautious
(h) enormous

Exercise 37

(a) agreeable
(b) illegible
(c) visible
(d) durable
(e) flexible
(f) adjustable

Exercise 38

(a) binary
(b) machinery
(c) necessary
(d) contemporary
(e) periphery
(f) delivery
(g) primary

Exercise 39

(a) extension
(b) distribution
(c) repulsion
(d) transmission
(e) restriction
(f) construction

Exercise 40

(a) proceed
(b) supersede
(c) precede
(d) succeed

Exercise 41

(a) ascertain
(b) miscellaneous
(c) conscious
(d) discipline
(e) artificial
(f) official
(g) essential
(h) initial

Grammar

Exercise 42

(a) Non-sentence
Force and inertia are related concepts in physics.

(b) Non-sentence
There are worms and insects that survive in the soil.

(c) Sentence
Subject: John Stuart Mill
Verb: realized

(d) Sentence
Subject: it
Verb: follows

(e) Non-sentence
There is a natural cycle for every element needed for life, each with its own natural circulation rate.

(f) Non-sentence
Pollution may result from getting rid of wastes at the least possible cost.

(g) Sentence
Subject: Gaseous emissions
Verb: may become

(h) Non-sentence
A way was found of generating electric currents from mechanical motion and hence of converting mechanical energy to electrical.

(i) Sentence
Subject: The rate
Verb: has been determined

(j) Non-sentence
In the process of cracking, large molecules are broken down into smaller ones by means of high temperatures and pressures.

(k) Non-sentence
Intensification of farming leads to soil deterioration and eventually erosion.

(l) Sentence
Subject: it
Verb: seems

Exercise 43

(a) 'Consists in' should be 'consists of'.
(b) 'Than my batteries', should be 'when my batteries'.
(c) Will you join me for a pint?
(d) 'Protest at' should be 'protest against'.
(e) 'Judged on' should be either 'judged by' or preferably 'judged according to'.

Exercise 44

(a) He is afraid of George and *me*.
(b) Correct
(c) He gave it to both me and *him*.
(d) Between you and *me*, he probably won't come.
(e) Correct

Exercise 45

(a) The amount of viscosity exhibited by different fluids *varies*.

(b) So much water and oil *have* been drawn from underground that the resources are much depleted.

(c) A library of subroutines *contributes* to the value of a computer installation in much the same way as an extra piece of equipment would do.

(d) The limitation of exhaust emissions and atmospheric pollution generally by the application of smoke control regulations *is* a further step in the improvement of the road-user's environment.

(e) This sentence is correct.

Exercise 46

(a) 'Ever' is unnecessary.   (d) 'About' is unnecessary.
(b) 'Of' is unnecessary.   (e) 'Up' is unnecessary.
(c) 'Being' is unnecessary.

Exercise 47

(a) This sentence is difficult to rearrange, and a better solution is to replace 'what' with 'why': Why have you given it to me?

(b) I was envious of their new house.
Although this is a solution, some of the emphasis of the original is lost.

(c) The 'to' is unnecessary.
When I began the journey, I was unsure where I was going.

Exercise 48

(a) affected   (c) effect
(b) affect   (d) effected

Exercise 49

In (a) the quiet running will be influenced (perhaps to be less quiet, perhaps more) by the adjustment. In (b) the quiet running will result from the adjustment.

Exercise 50

(a) The bar graph is used to represent data that *are* either nominally or ordinally scaled.

(b) It is easy to work out the circumference of a circle once the length of a *radius* is known.

(c) If neither of these experimental methods *is* successful you must try a third one.

(d) The committee *were* divided in their opinions.

(e) In your assignments you may write 'none is' or 'none are'; either *is* acceptable.

(f) Adding the *indices* is a method of multiplication used in mathematics.

(g) Each of the units of measurement *was* originally *a* natural *unit* based on the *length* of *a* certain *part* of the human hand or foot.
Or:
All the units of measurement were originally natural units based on the lengths of certain parts of the human hand or foot.

(h) The action of *bacteria breaks* down the carbon compounds of plant systems to carbon dioxide and water.

(i) In a White Paper of 1970 a network of motorways for England of 4200 miles *was* proposed.

(j) What is your *criterion* for making such a judgement?
Or:
What *are* your criteria for making such a judgement?

(k) This sentence is correct.

(l) *Both* distribution through microwave radio links using tall towers *and* transmission from a satellite far above the surface of the earth are possible ways of disseminating television.
Or:
Either distribution through micro-wave radio links using tall towers or transmission from a satellite far above the surface of the earth *is a* possible *way* of disseminating television.

Exercise 51

(a)	practice	(h)	principle
(b)	principal	(i)	compliment
(c)	practised	(j)	defuse
(d)	complement	(k)	stationery
(e)	diffuse	(l)	stationary
(f)	discreet	(m)	proceeded
(g)	precedes	(n)	discrete

Exercise 52

(a) Only I spoke to my tutor yesterday.
Meaning: I was the one person who spoke to my tutor yesterday.

(b) I only spoke to my tutor yesterday.
Meaning: I did not see my tutor, I spoke to him yesterday.

(c) I spoke only to my tutor yesterday.
Meaning: I spoke to my tutor yesterday, but not to anyone else.

(d) I spoke to my only tutor yesterday.
Meaning: I have just one tutor, to whom I spoke yesterday.

(e) I spoke to my tutor only yesterday.
Meaning: I spoke to my tutor as recently as yesterday.

(f) I spoke to my tutor yesterday only.
Meaning: The one day on which I spoke to my tutor was yesterday.

Note. You may have felt the meanings indicated above are different from the ones you have given. The intonation, or speed and stress, in reading the sentences may alter the interpretation; versions besides those given may be correct. The important thing is for you to realize how much the sense may be altered by 'minor' rearrangement of words in a sentence.

Exercise 53

(a) Although the shark-spotting helicopter was circling over the bathers it apparently failed to see the shark.

(b) This sentence is confusing and subject to many interpretations; here is one:
As the guard went about his duties, the man watched him closely, noting the time he came to feed the prisoner.

(c) Again this is open to various interpretations:
I told my mother that she should help the woman.

(d) If the baby doesn't thrive on raw milk, boil the milk.

(e) In my desk there are some sticking plasters, which I keep for emergencies.

Exercise 54

(a) fewer
(b) comprised
(c) lay

Exercise 55

(a) Correct. Rule three, therefore *whom*: to (preposition) whom.

(b) Incorrect. Rule three, therefore *whom*: from (preposition) whom.

(c) Incorrect. Rule one, therefore *who*: who is illiterate. 'It appears' is, as it were, in brackets.

(d) Correct. Rule two, therefore *whom*: we thought whom (object) to be trustworthy.

(e) Incorrect. Rule one, therefore *who*: who is coming to tea? 'Do you suppose' is, as it were, in brackets.

Exercise 56

(a) specific variations in the design of a system that uses diesel fuel
Or:
variations in the design of a specific system that uses diesel fuel

(b) *Possibly*: a network (?) for the exchange of information

(c) a programme for the improvement of domestic accommodation (i.e. housing)

Exercise 57

(a) We thank you for your order and, being always anxious to carry out our customers' wishes immediately, *we ask if you would* kindly state the address to which you wish the goods to be delivered.

(b) Whilst requesting you to furnish the return now outstanding *we advise you* that in future no further credit will be extended.

(c) *It was* administered at first by the National Gallery; *in* 1917 the appointment of a separate board and director enabled a fully independent policy to be pursued.

(d) Arising out of a confrontation between the Government and the Opposition over devolution, *an early vote of no confidence in the Government may be sought by Mrs Thatcher.*

Exercise 58

(a) It is difficult with this example because 'scarcely' should have been matched with the positive verb 'was'. Logically interpreted it would be:
He was quite able to read the unit.

(b) '*I did say something,*' she protested.

(c) This suggests that the solution could be worked with difficulty:
It's *just about a workable* solution.

(d) This implies that there was some compulsion to go; it was not possible to refuse. Perhaps it is best rewritten as:
I *was obliged to* go.

(e) *Everyone* in this room *has* sometimes lied.

Exercise 59

(a) It is the intention of the Minister of Transport to increase substantially all present rates by means of a general percentage.

(b) We intend to support further attempts at obtaining a truce.
Or:
We intend to continue to support attempts at obtaining a truce.

Note. Although the sentence, 'We intend to support further attempts at obtaining a truce' is grammatically correct, its meaning is not clear. In this version 'further' could apply to either 'support' or to 'attempts'; from the sentence given originally we know that it relates to 'support'.

(c) He still seems to be allowed to speak at unionist demonstrations.

(d) The greatest difficulty about assessing the economic achievements of the Soviet Union is that its spokesmen try to exaggerate them absurdly.

(e) Many of the workers are said to favour strongly a strike.

(f) It will be possible to improve considerably the wages of the workers.

Exercise 60

(a) I was late with my assignment because I found the calculations difficult, and so I didn't know whether my tutor would mark it.

(b) The Prime Minister said that she hoped that everyone would cooperate with the new pay agreement. Her backbenchers went on to give the scheme their unqualified support.

(c) If there is anything more I can do in the next few weeks to further the project, I will do it.

Exercise 61

(a) etc.   (d) e.g.
(b) i.e.   (e) i.e.
(c) i.e.

Exercise 62

(a) Omit *to try*, it is contained in *attempt*.
(b) Change to: The mortar will possibly crack.
(c) Omit *in the past*.
(d) Omit *in shape*, it is implied in square.
(e) Omit *about*, or omit *The subject of*.
(f) Change *because* to *that*.

Exercise 63

(a) Competition encourages cheap production and so helps to control prices.

(b) The various unions which represent the tool-shop workers disagreed strongly.

(c) There was a useful discussion of the matters presented by the dockers' negotiator.

(d) As a result of careful investigation the depot has been designed to take both road and rail freight.

(e) The two leaders will meet once.

(f) They discussed an article which examined the place of the green pound in British agriculture.

(g) Each borrower will make yearly repayments that relate to his income.

(h) When investing money one must consider the future.

(i) British agriculture must be ready to respond to home and overseas demand and to help improve the national income.

(j) I wanted to make a profit; the Board did not.

Exercise 64

(a) By looking at current trends we can estimate likely future developments.

(b) Animals, plants and soils are distributed in zones; because of mobility of animals the boundaries of their zones are the least distinct.

Exercise 65

(a) The Chancellor announced that the country was becoming more optimistic as a result of the stronger economy.

(b) The shop steward stated publicly that the management's refusal to negotiate was only the beginning of the matter.

(c) If irresponsible wage claims made for rapid inflation, Britain would suffer.

(d) You will often encounter examples of narrow specialism, where problems have been solved in a limited context without a look at the wider consequences of the solutions or the ways used to achieve them.

(e) Under the Race Relations Act, such tests could be challenged for the first time as a form of indirect discrimination.

Exericse 66

(a) Winds do not explode; they may destroy or devastate. 'Wind' does not make clear what is happening to the currency.

(b) An abstract notion like 'flexibility' cannot also be a corner-stone.

(c) It's difficult to think of something concrete coming out of an olive branch, so this mixed metaphor adds nothing to our understanding.

(d) The image of something concrete and lifeless is combined with an image of a living thing. It is not clear what impression the writer is trying to make on the reader.

Exercise 67

(a) (ii) A chronic illness is long lasting. 'Severe' would be a better word to use in (i).

(b) (ii) 'Allergic' is a medical term which describes the condition of a patient who is sensitive to some substance that is normally harmless. It could be allowed in (i) that it is a metaphorical description of a possible reaction to filling in forms.

(c) (i) 'Facilitate' means to make easy or help forward. In (ii) it is used as if it meant 'given the services of' or 'assisted by'. It was the research that was facilitated, not the student.

(d) (ii) To anticipate something is to forestall it, to act as if it has already taken place. It does not mean the same as 'to expect'.

Exercise 68

(a) A man of his weight would break such a flimsy chair.
'Of his proportions' is a cliché; the word 'weight' is simpler and clearer to the reader.

(b) I have received your letter of the 4th and will be replying as soon as I have any information for you.
'Am in receipt of your letter of 4th inst.' is an example of office jargon; the revised version is a more natural way of expressing the sense of the original phrase.

(c) This sentence is correct; '*in camera*' is used in its specific sense of 'not held in public'.

(d) There is every indication that the new corporation will be very successful.
'Tower of strength' and 'forge ahead' are mixed metaphors. They have little impact on the reader and the one suggests immobility, the other movement.

(e) These investigations will be an essential contribution to the process of assessing market trends.
'Input' is a sloppy use here of a technical term from computer language.

(f) Please use this form.
This is probably what the writer meant in plain English.

(g) The bankruptcy of Rolls-Royce shocked the nation.
'Trauma' is a sloppy use of a technical term. 'Real precedent' is a cliché. The revised version is simpler and clearer to the reader.

Bibliographies and references

Exercise 69

A bibliography is a list of books giving details of their authorship, editions, etc. By extension a bibliography can include other printed items that are not strictly books, for example, papers published in learned journals.

Exercise 70

(a) K.R. Clew, *The Kennet & Avon Canal*, David & Charles, 1968.
(b) M.E. Solomon, *Population Dynamics*, Edward Arnold, 1969.
(c) M.P. Crosland (ed.), *The Science of Matter*, Penguin, 1971.

Exercise 72

(a) Rothschild, 'Risk', *Listener*, vol. 100, no. 2588, 30 November 1978, pp. 715–18.

(b) (i) D. Nicholls, 'Theories of acids and bases', *Chemistry Student*, vol. 1, no. 2, 1967, pp. 33–8.
(ii) D. Nicholls, 'Theories of acids and bases', reprinted in J.G. Stark (ed.), *Modern Chemistry*, Penguin, 1970, pp. 191–204.

Exercise 73

W. Alexander and A. Street, *Metals in the Service of Man* (3rd edn), Penguin, 1946.

G. Boyle, D. Elliottt and R. Roy (eds.), *The Politics of Technology*, Longman/The Open University Press, 1977.

T.K. Derry and T.I. Williams, *A Short History of Technology* (paperback edn), Oxford University Press, 1970.

B.M. Glauert, *Principles of Dynamics*, Routledge & Kegan Paul, 1960.

M.F. Hoyaux, 'Plasma physics and its applications', *Contemporary Physics*, vol. 7, no. 4, 1966, pp. 241–60.

R.L. Kovach, 'Earthquake prediction and modification', in I.G. Gass, P.J. Smith and R.C.L. Wilson (eds.), *Understanding the Earth* (2nd edn), Artemis Press/The Open University Press, 1972, pp. 327–32.

R. Parsons, 'Electrolysis and simple cells', *Contemporary Physics*, vol. 10, no. 3, 1969, pp. 205–20.

Bibliography

Plain English could not have been prepared without the help of many books whose aim is to help the writing of plain English. Those that were most frequently referred to are listed here, with a few others that you may find helpful. The dictionaries listed are just a selection. I have added notes about those books that are most likely to be of interest to you, should you wish to pursue your study of writing good English.

Books

R. Barrass, *Scientists Must Write*, Chapman & Hall, 1978.

G.V. Carey, *Mind the Stop*, Penguin, 1971.
An excellent, inexpensive guide to punctuation.

D.J. Collinson, *Writing English*, Pan, 1982.

H.W. Fowler, *Modern English Usage*, 2nd edn, rev. E. Gowers, Oxford University Press, 1965.

E. Gowers, *The Complete Plain Words*, 2nd edn, rev. B. Fraser, Penguin, 1973.
Originally written for civil servants, this book is an excellent guide for anyone who is concerned about writing clearly. The title of *Plain English* reflects its indebtedness to this book.

R.E. Morsberger, *Common Sense Grammar and Style*, Thomas Y. Cromwell, 1972.

E. Partridge, *Usage and Abusage*, rev. edn, Penguin, 1969.

C.W. Ryan, *Spelling for Adults*, Wiley, 1973.

H.J. Tichy, *Effective Writing for Engineers – Managers – Scientists*, Wiley, 1966.

C. Turk and J. Kirkman, *Effective Writing*, Spon, 1982.

G.H. Vallins, *Good English*, Pan, 1951.

Dictionaries

New or revised editions of these dictionaries are published quite frequently. The following list was up to date at the time of printing (1983).

Chambers Everyday Dictionary, rev. edn, Chambers, 1979 (also available as a paperback).

Chambers 20th Century Dictionary, new edn, Chambers, 1983.

Collins Concise English Dictionary, new edn, Collins, 1982.

Concise Oxford Dictionary, 7th edn, Oxford University Press, 1982.

Longman New Universal Dictionary, Longman, 1982.

Oxford Paperback Dictionary, 2nd edn, Oxford University Press, 1983.

Penguin English Dictionary, 3rd edn, Penguin, 1979 (paperback; also available as a hardback).

Pocket Oxford Dictionary, 6th edn, Oxford University Press, 1978.

Living with Technology

Within each block the mainstream title is given first and the tributary titles follow.

Introduction

Block 1 Home
Block 1 Numeracy
Block 1 Space and Comfort
Block 1 Heat
Block 1 Structures and Materials

Block 2 Communication
Block 2 Numeracy
Block 2 Electricity
Block 2 Signals
Block 2 Feedback
Block 2 Computers

Block 3 Energy
Block 3 Numeracy
Block 3 Energy Conversion

Block 4 Resources
Block 4 Numeracy
Block 4 Chemistry
Block 4 Materials

Block 5 Food
Block 5 Biology
Block 5 Chemistry

Block 6 Health
Block 6 Numeracy

Plain English